Human Experience of God

Denis Edwards

HUMAN EXPERIENCE OF GOD

PAULIST PRESS
New York/Ramsey

Library of Congress
Catalog Card Number: 83-62464

ISBN: 0-8091-2559-5

Published by Paulist Press
545 Island Road, Ramsey, N.J. 07446

Printed and bound in the
United States of America

contents

for Kath and Mark Edwards

PREFACE

In the early Church, and in the writing of the medieval thinkers, theology and religious experience are intimately linked. In the work of Thomas Aquinas there is a profound integration of Christian experience and rational reflection. However, after Thomas, we find the development of a dogmatic theology which is independent of religious experience and somewhat suspicious of it, and a tradition of mystical experience and mystical theology which is not well grounded in a broader theology. In our own time we are confronted with the urgent task of building a theological approach to human experience of God. Karl Rahner, more than any other writer, has enabled Catholic theology to move in this direction. As will be evident from the footnotes, this book depends upon Rahner's thought at several stages. However it also depends upon many others—Augustine and Aquinas, the mystical tradition of the Church, and the insights of contemporary theologians and Scripture scholars.

I owe thanks to many people. First to Avery Dulles, S.J. for teaching me much about the theologian's craft, and for graciously agreeing to write an introduction to this book. Then there are those who read the manuscript and offered helpful suggestions: John Wilken, S.J., John Thornhill, S.M., Christine Burke I.B.V.M., Augustine Fitzsimons, C.P. and Patricia Fox R.S.M. They, of course, are not responsible for inadequacies left in the text. I owe a large debt to all those who have struggled with me over the issue of experience of God in theology classes in Adelaide. Finally I owe much to those who have helped type and retype the manuscript: Liz Kenny, Marie Reitano, Mary Conradi, and Julia Wenham.

INTRODUCTION

In Catholic Christianity it is generally recognized that God is knowable in two distinct ways: by faith and by reason. He is known by faith when we acknowledge his reality on the basis of testimony—his own testimony to himself that comes to us through Scripture and the tradition of the believing community. God is said to be knowable by reason insofar as his existence and attributes can be inferred from the qualities of the created universe. The philosophical proofs of God's existence are attempts to state in rigorous form what is grasped in an imprecise, informal, and spontaneous way by untrained minds.

Granted that God is knowable in these two ways, the question arises whether and in what sense human beings have an "experience" of God. Since God is not an object in the world but a reality transcending all actual and possible objects, it is evident that any experience we have of God must be quite different in character from the experience of stones, tables, or other human persons. God transcends not only all objects but every human knower, and thus the self-experience of the knowing subject is not the same as an experience of God. Since God is neither the subject nor the object of human experience, it is no easy matter to explain how he can be experienced. And yet an increasing number of theologians, with whom Denis Edwards aligns himself, assert that in some sense we do experience God. God is present all the time, acting upon us as conscious beings. Can we not say, then, that our vital and immediate contact with God can, at least in faith, be called an experience of God?

The Bible seems to suggest that at least some human persons have a fleeting and tenuous experience of the divine. To the Israelites it was axiomatic that no one could see God face to face and live (Ex 33:20). Yet God is said to have spoken to Moses "face to face, as a man speaks to his friend" (Ex 33:11). On one occasion God is said to have permitted Moses to see his back as he disappeared into the distance (Ex 33:23).

Throughout the New Testament it is asserted that God himself has come among us visibly in Jesus Christ and invisibly in the Holy Spirit. The apostles are convinced that in Jesus they have seen and touched "the word of life" (1 Jn 1:1). They teach that the Holy Spirit, although remaining enveloped in mystery (cf. Jn 3:8), gives testimony to our spirit that we are children of God (Rom 8:16; Gal 4:6). But the New Testament also asserts that God dwells in inaccessible light (1 Tim 6:16). He is known in an obscure way through faith (2 Cor 5:6; cf. 1 Cor 13:12) and by inference from the created world (Rom 1:20). Whatever experience we have of God, therefore, does not make faith or reason unnecessary.

Down through the centuries the Catholic theological tradition has grappled with the question of the human experience of God. In descriptions of the mystical experience some authors seem to speak as though the divine presence makes itself palpable at certain privileged moments. Yet a great spiritual theologian such as Anselm draws a sharp contrast between his conviction that God is immediately present and his inability to experience God. "You are within me and around me," he writes, "and I feel you not" (*Proslogium*, chap. 16).

Thomas Aquinas is an eminent authority on our question. In his discussion of the gifts of the Holy Spirit, and especially of wisdom, he says that those who have the theological virtue of charity are gifted with the Holy Spirit and are thereby endowed with a certain connaturality with "divine things." Such persons, says St. Thomas, are united to God through love (*Summa theol.* 2-2, q. 45, a. 2). This loving union might seem to imply an experience of God. Yet when he treats the question whether we can know by experience that we are in a state of grace, Thomas answers in the negative. He holds that since grace is not a constituent of our being, we cannot perceive it experientially. Our experiences of consolation in living according to the Gospel can permit us to conjecture that we are in God's grace (*Summa theol.* 1-2, q. 112, a. 5). Thus Thomas Aquinas does not seem to say explicitly that we have an experience of God.

Since the issue of the human experience of God is an important one and is still in need of clarification, we are fortunate to have the thorough and solid treatment that Denis Edwards provides in the present volume. While acknowledging the elusive nature of God's presence, Edwards takes a firm position that we do experience God. He builds his argument principally on passages from St. John of the Cross and Karl Rahner, two authors he has studied in depth. He also relies on the "reconstructed" theory of experience that has been worked out by contemporary philosophers such as John E. Smith.

In contending for the human experience of God, Edwards makes careful distinctions. He does not hold that the experience is a pre-suppositionless one or one that occurs independently of one's subjective attitudes. Rather he holds that the experience presupposes a God-given dynamism of the human spirit toward God, the absolute transcendent. Edwards is also conscious that this experience becomes sharper and more intense in a community of faith, and that apart from the preaching of the Gospel we could not recognize even our most blessed moments as encounters with God. Christian doctrine enables us to name what we previously knew only in a vague, implicit way.

The experience of God, for Edwards, necessarily occurs within an experience of worldly objects, and is in a sense mediated by these. Unless we have been taught to interpret the signs we cannot discern God in them. The experience of God is normally shaped in a community of religious faith. What Edwards says about the God-experience is, in an analogous way, true of other rich and rewarding experiences. Only a person who has been trained in the appropriate disciplines can appreciate great literature. Only a person formed in a sports-loving community can enjoy the thrill of a championship match. The experience of an historic event occurring in our own lifetime is shot through with many elements of inference and interpretation. The Church, with its tradition, provides the interpretative context in which religious signs and sacraments are experienced as embodiments and manifestations of God's real presence to us and to our world.

In recognizing the interpretative character of all meaningful experience Edwards distances himself from the view of certain mystical empiricists who have maintained that human beings can have a direct, unmediated experience of God at certain privileged moments. This position seems unacceptable because God cannot possibly appear as an object. Every object must be viewed against some larger horizon, but God himself is the ultimate horizon. Since the experience of God is non-objective, it must, for Edwards, be obscure.

As I hope these introductory remarks have shown, the present book is a serious contribution to an ongoing debate in which the questions have been progressively refined by acute theological reflection. But I would not wish to give the impression that this is a heavy philosophical treatise, written only for a small class of scholars. On the contrary, it is a very down to earth and practical book, filled with applications to the life-situations of ordinary believers. Denis Edwards writes as a priest who has had considerable experience in religious education and in spiritual direction. He is sensitive to the problems both of marginal Christians and of believers seeking to achieve a more intense life of prayer.

Particularly valuable, in my opinion, are the sections of

this book in which, with the help of John of the Cross, it treats of contemplative prayer, and those in which, with the help of Karl Rahner, it takes up the question of "discernment of spirits" in the decision-making process. In dealing with this latter question Edwards makes excellent use of the *Spiritual Exercises* of Ignatius of Loyola—a work which he confessedly interprets according to the mind of Rahner. Readers of this work should be aware that St. Ignatius himself does not speak explicitly of the human experience of God, nor do all commentators agree that such an experience is even implicitly referred to. Yet the recent work of Harvey Egan, to which Fr. Edwards refers, makes a convincing case that St. Ignatius, especially in his Spiritual Journal, must be interpreted as holding that God can be perceived as immediately communicating himself to the human spirit.

The pastoral and spiritual dimensions of this book, in my opinion, enhance its value precisely as a work of theology. Fr. Edwards provides strong reasons for holding that good theology is always closely related to the spiritual life. If this book is even partially correct, God is best known not through dry conceptual discourse but through loving, prayerful union. The gap that has developed since the sixteenth century between doctrinal theology (as something rigorously conceptual and scientific) and spiritual theology (as a practical and hortatory discipline) has done harm to both theology and spirituality. Readers will be grateful to Fr. Edwards for helping to bridge this unfortunate gap and thus to restore the idea of a Christian theology that takes proper account of worship, prayer, and the struggle to live according to the Gospel.

Avery Dulles, S.J.

one

WHY SPEAK OF "EXPERIENCE OF GOD"?

The Need for a Theology of Experience of God

Do we have "experience of God"? Is this a legitimate way of speaking about our relationship with God? If we do speak of "experience of God" what kind of experience do we mean?

The answers to these questions are far from obvious. Yet there are few questions that are more important to the men and women of the late twentieth century, whether they be unbelievers, marginal Christians or committed Christians. It takes only a little reflection to see that an adequate theology of experience of God is necessary for effective ministry to each of these groups. Perhaps the best way to show this is by describing four individuals. Each of them, it seems to me, represents a large section of our community.

Julia is a young woman approaching thirty. She finds herself doubting the existence of God. At some times she is inclined to believe in "something" but at other times she thinks of herself as a non-believer, an atheist. Julia was brought up as a Christian and admits to having picked up from her religious background some important values, including a sense of justice. She is generous and compassionate in the way she lives her life, but the word "God" and the language of the Church mean little to her. The Church's idea of God seems far-fetched and

1

alien. It fails to connect with anything which is within the range of her experience. Julia's commitment to social issues is still strong, but she finds within herself an emptiness and an obscure hunger for something more. She knows that she has a need for depth and meaning, but she cannot be satisfied with superficial answers. A properly developed theology of experience of God will have some hope of speaking to those who, like Julia, hold an agnostic position. Instead of rational argument for God's existence (which rarely convinces anyone) this approach would suggest to Julia that she search into her own experience of life, to see if moments of mystery and transcendence can be found there. At this point real dialogue with Julia might begin.

A second set of questions is posed today by the great number of people like Margaret. She finds Christianity irrelevant to her life. Margaret's husband left her six years ago. She has three children, the eldest of them just out of school and unemployed. They live in government housing in one of the poorest parts of the city, where she fears for her children because of the violence of the neighborhood, the gangs that roam the streets and the access to drugs of all kinds. Financial survival is a constant preoccupation and she lives without much hope that life will change for the better. She feels that there is nothing left for her, that she has failed, and she finds herself overwhelmed by bouts of loneliness. Margaret has not abandoned the Church completely but the doctrines and liturgy of the Church have little meaning for her. What matters for her is what she experiences each day: the battle to survive, the daily round of work, her hope that her son will find a job, the endurance of loneliness and her hunger for companionship, a hunger that often is met only by the television set. Any kind of pastoral analysis reveals that there are enormous numbers of Christians (many of them in circumstances different from Margaret's) who experience this chasm between what makes up their lives and the faith language of the Church. An adequate understanding of experience of God is, I believe, the only bridge over the chasm. The necessary mediation between personal experience and the language and practice of the Church is the discovery of the depths of what one is experiencing, and the further discovery that these depths open out into the mystery of God. Once this journey of discovery begins the language of the tradition may again have a point of contact with the experience of the person.

Margaret might well be described as a marginal Christian. Like many others she is marginal in terms of her identifcation with the local church. She is also marginal in terms of society. She is among the poorest and the most hurt. People like Margaret force us to ask ourselves what connection there is between the eucharistic assemblies of Christians and the pain of so many in our world. This question can never receive an adequate answer, except in the cross of Jesus, and this answer remains mysterious. However I want to suggest that one response that ought to be made to this problem is by way of the theology of experience of God, in the link between our experience of those who are pushed to the margins in our world and our experience of God.

Tom, unlike Julia and Margaret, is a Christian committed to his local parish and to Sunday Eucharist. He has worked hard all his life and he and his wife have watched their children leave home to begin their own families. As he begins his retirement from work he finds his life empty. He has high blood pressure and is becoming increasingly conscious that he is in the last stage of life and that his own death must be faced. Tom believes that God exists, that this God has been revealed to us in Jesus Christ, that the Church teaches in the name of Jesus and that we are transformed by God's grace. However he has always believed that grace operates at a level beyond anything he might experience. His faith has always been largely a matter of intellectual assent. Now, as Tom faces the bleak emptiness of his life, his failing health and the possibility of death, his own kind of faith has little to offer him. It makes no connections with his own struggle. He has no access to the richness and joy of a more personal faith that could lead him to wisdom and to peace, and the capacity to love more creatively. A theology of experience of God has some hope of suggesting to Tom, and all those like him, that God does reach out to us in love individually and that there is a way to a more affective and personal faith.

Trevor is also committed to the Church, but his faith has a character entirely different from that of Tom. A family man in his early forties, Trevor recently went through a remarkable conversion experience. In his own language he "found God" and he found Christian community in a charismatic prayer group. All his earlier Church life seems like nothing compared to his new experience. Trevor now speaks easily and often of God and gives the impression of having easy access to him. He believes that God is manifested to those with faith and on different occasions he claims to be directly guided by God in his decisions. Trevor, like many others, has a tendency to identify uncritically his own religious enthusiasm with God, without any awareness that his own psychic state may be contributing to what he experiences. A theological approach to experience of God will offer Trevor a caution against losing sight of the transcendence of God. It will provide a framework for Trevor's experience in the spiritual tradition of the Church. It will show the inner connection between prayerful experience of God and an active engagement in the struggle for justice. Finally, it will offer some guidelines for discernment between genuine experience of God and other human experiences.

There is, then, an urgent need for a theology of experience of God in order that we be able to respond to some of the important questions of our time. I would suggest, as well, that it is only by developing such a theology that we can be faithful to our tradition. Only an adequate theology of experience of God can do justice to the Old and New Testament understanding that God breaks in on our individual lives, that the Spirit moves within us, that God's Word is communicated to us, and that we live in God's presence.[1] Such a theological approach to experience of God can be shown to stand in the tradition of Augustine and Aquinas,[2] and while this tradition may have been obscured in the excessive rationalism of some post-Reformation Scholastic theology, it has always been remembered by the mystics. Without a theology of the experience of God we can make no sense of the works of John of the Cross and the *Spiritual Exercises* of St. Ignatius have no content.

It should be noticed, too, that we cannot develop a theology of revelation which is not built upon an understanding of our experience of God. If one denies all possibility of encounter with God, then the possibility of revelation is either denied or reduced to something entirely extrinsic.

In the project of developing a theology of experience of God careful use of language is extremely important. What do we mean when we use the word "experience" in this context? And what do we mean when we claim that such experience is "of God"? There is a tradition in theology which is hesitant to speak of the human experience of God. There are important reasons for this. One of them is the need to preserve God's transcendence, and any theological language that fails to safeguard this transcendence is automatically and rightly suspect. Where experience is taken to mean the same thing as knowledge or comprehension, then the phrase "experience of God" is rightly called into question. I hope to make clear that experience and conceptual knowledge are not the same thing. It is possible to show that while we do not have access to God's inner being, and while God always transcends our intellectual comprehension, yet we can and do experience the presence and activity of this Holy One in a pre-conceptual way.

If we must speak of experience of God, then it is essential

that we clarify what is meant, and is not meant, by the phrase. The first step in this will be an examination of "experience" itself. Then there will be need to show that there are some experiences which are of a pre-conceptual nature. Finally there will be a need to discuss what is meant by the expression "experience of God" as distinct from other common expressions like "religious experience."

The Nature of Experience

It might be helpful to begin an examination of the nature of experience through a reflection about our experience of another person in our lives. What do we mean when we say that we have some experience of this person? Usually we mean (1) that we have had one or more encounters with the person, and (2) that we have formed some kind of interpretation or understanding of this person as a result of these encounters.

First, then, we mean that we have encountered the other person. We would not normally claim to have experience of another person unless we have had some kind of meeting with him or her, even if the meeting occurs only through a telephone call or a letter.

Second, we mean that we have interpreted these meetings within our own consciousness, and that we now have some understanding of the other person as a result of our encounters with him or her. There is no real experience of another unless we become aware of the encounter. We have to interpret to ourselves the person we encounter by way of images and concepts. Even after speaking with someone on the telephone we form an interpretation of the person encountered through the tone of voice, the warm or cold manner and the accent of the person, as well as by the content of what was said. We have some kind of understanding of the person on the other end of the line. There are many other routine encounters, like sitting next to a person on a bus, which may not deserve to be called experience of another, because we have not really received the other person into our own consciousness in any way.

Experience, then, involves both encounter and the interpretation of the encounter. There is always the reflective, conceptual awareness of what we experience, but this points back to the original experiential encounter.

It is important to stress this double dimension in experience because it is not always noticed. Sometimes people speak of experience as if it involved only encounters with others, and they forget the role their own consciousness has played in selecting and filtering what is received. Others stress only the subjective side and forget that genuine experience depends upon a real meeting with some reality beyond the individual.

Experience is best seen as encounter with some thing or person which has become available to consciousness through reflective awareness. It refers to an encounter that is interpreted within human consciousness. This second element, interpretation, has always already occurred whenever we know that we have experienced something.[3]

However the interpretative element in experience should not be seen as something that occurs only after an encounter, in a moment of reflection. Rather the individual brings to an encounter a receptivity, or lack of it, which has been determined by the person's capabilities, free choices and previous experience. Two people may hear a man describe his difficulties in his relationship with his wife. The first person sees the man as arrogant and self-centered while the second feels empathy and understanding for him. Both have had a similar encounter with him but they have experienced him quite differently. Their own previous experience and their present state of mind have determined how they have received this man. The interpreting self precedes the encounter, enters into the encounter, and reflects upon the encounter.

Even though my original experience of a person can only be present to me through my reflection upon it, it is possible, as I reflect, to distinguish my conceptual understanding from the original encounter. I may become quite aware that my thoughts about a person are inadequate reflections of the original encounter. In fact it is true to say that any real encounter with the humanity of another person has an element of mystery which escapes my comprehension. Not only does my reflection on an encounter with another person enable me to distinguish the encounter from the subsequent interpretation of it, but it also reveals that the original encounter was richer than my reflective conceptual awareness and contained something that escapes rational expression.

The American philosopher John E. Smith speaks of experience as "a product of the intersection of something encountered and a being capable of interpreting the results."[4] This is a good working description of experience. It stresses the two moments of encounter and of interpretation. It makes it clear that both the original encounter and the act of interpretation are essential and necessarily linked together.

The use of the concepts of encounter and interpretation in a description of experience preserves our understanding of experience from distortion.[5] One distortion of experience is to see it as an entirely subjective process, quite unreliable when compared with scientific measurement or logical thought. Those who hold this view of experience dismiss it as unreliable and at the mercy of the whims and prejudices of the individual. The concept of experience as the product of an intersection or an encounter makes it clear that experience has its objective side. The reality encountered, the person who is having the experience, and the actual meeting between the two are clearly objective realities. At the heart of experience is the moment of encounter which is quite objective.

However, experience certainly has its subjective side as

well. The concept of experience as an encounter which yet needs interpretation allows that the original encounter has to receive concrete life in a person through the mediation of the person's reflective consciousness. In the interpretative stage of experience there may be distortion because of the biases of an individual, because of dishonesty, because of emotional blockages, because of unconscious motives, or because what has been experienced is too much for a person's ability to conceptualize and express it. However, a human person is capable of checking biases, becoming aware of self-deceptions, admitting limitations and thereby reducing the probability of mistakes or distortion in interpretation of experience.

Awareness of the way the individual enters into the experience (in the interpretation of what is encountered) introduces a critical note into our concept of experience. There is always the need to be critically aware of the way a person's subjectivity shapes his or her reception of experience. At the same time it is important to insist that there is an objective basis to experience in the original encounter, in the person who is experiencing and in what is encountered.

Pre-Conceptual Experiences

There are several different ways in which we experience reality. The most immediate and obvious experiences are those of the five senses. We experience a rose through sight and smell and perhaps through touch. Even much more complex experiences, such as our encounter with another human person, depend upon a basis in the senses. We see a person's facial expressions, or read his or her letters. We listen to a person's voice and so share his or her thoughts.

Needless to say, when we speak of experience of God we are not referring to such sense experience. Of course, experiences of the senses can lead us to a reflective awareness of God, and they can and do act as symbolic mediations of God's presence in our lives. This kind of mediation occurs in a unique way in the Church's sacraments. However, in accurate theological language the phrase "experience of God" means something other than sense experience.

A second way we encounter reality which is external to ourselves is through an intellectual grasp of it. An example of this is the experience we have in reading a book of theology. We are brought into contact with another person's ideas and grapple with them intellectually. We experience reality through concepts and rational judgments. We do this also when we read a newspaper, when we struggle with problems at work and when we engage in the simple interchange of everyday conversation. Such intellectual experience depends, of course, upon sense experience since we depend upon sight and hearing for intellectual encounters. However it is still accurate to speak of such encounters as intellectual experience of reality.

Now it is true that we can form concepts of God and the attributes of God and we can think about the nature of God. We must notice, however, that all of our thinking about God is analogical. We take some reality we know from our everyday world, such as goodness or fatherhood, and we attribute it to God. In doing this there is always the implied reservation that while God is rightly called good he is not good in the way human beings are good, but in a way that totally transcends human goodness. We can think about God, then, but our intellects can approach God only by way of analogy. This "only" is not meant to demean the importance of this kind of knowledge, but simply to point to its proper limits. God is by very definition incomprehensible, and the human intellect must know God as an abiding mystery to it. Our intellects, then, do not grasp God as he is in himself. He always transcends our concepts.

If we do not have sense experience of God and if he escapes the grasp of our intellects, does this mean that we can have no real experience of God at all? Many people would say that this is the case. However this is to ignore another whole area of human experience, the area that I will call pre-conceptual experience.

The philosopher and scientist Michael Polanyi has shown how much of our knowing occurs at what he calls a "tacit" level. He shows how a great deal of scientific research depends upon unspoken and non-conceptualized assumptions, presuppositions, skills and intuitions. No expert tradesperson can pass on skills to an apprentice simply in concepts or words. Much of what men and women who are gifted in a craft know can never be articulated. They know more then they can tell:

> Although the expert diagnostician, taxonomist and cotton-classer can indicate their clues and formulate their maxims, they know many more things than they can tell, knowing them only in practice, as instrumental particulars, and not explicitly, as objects.[6]

Polanyi shows how we operate with "tacit" or pre-conceptual knowledge in many ordinary areas of life. When a woman learns to ride a bicycle it is often impossible for her to explain to another (or herself) the nature of the skill. A man might be able to pick his own raincoat from fifty others at a function and yet be unable to describe it to another person.[7] In these and a thousand other ways we know more than we can tell.

There are other, deeper experiences that occur at a pre-conceptual level. When a man listens to a symphony he depends upon sense experience to hear the individual notes. He uses his intellect to grasp the conceptual order of the music and the interrelationship of part and whole. However he experiences a beauty which transcends the faculties of hearing and thought. The beauty of the symphony is beyond logic, and the man knows that what he experiences cannot adequately be reduced to concepts or words. When he reflects on the experience and tries to speak about it, he has to use concepts, images and words. However he knows that what he has experienced is beyond his ability to verbalize it. Such an experience of beauty is pre-conceptual.

When a woman loves another person, she knows that her love is built upon sense experience of the other and upon an intellectual meeting with him or her. But again the mystery of the other person and the mystery of the love that is shared escapes comprehension. It transcends the senses and the intellect. It can be conceptualized and it can be verbalized (and needs to be verbalized if it is to reach its full human potential) but she knows that her words are inadequate and point to a reality that she despairs of properly expressing. Such love is experienced in a pre-conceptual way.

These two examples, beauty and love, reveal something important to us about our experience. Both experiences depend upon the senses and the intellect but they both transcend the senses and the intellect. They reveal a level of experience which is central to human life and yet one which we cannot intellectually dominate. Such pre-conceptual experiences do become conceptualized and verbalized as we interpret them for ourselves. However, we are quite able to distinguish between our conceptual interpretation, which we know is inadequate, and the original pre-conceptual experience.

There are many other such experiences, some of which will be discussed later. However, even a preliminary reflection on the experiences of beauty and love is enough to show that some of our deepest experiences, and those that we would list as most central to what it is to be human, occur in a pre-conceptual way. This reflection shows how dangerous is the superficial empirical attitude which reduces what is experienced to the senses and what can be measured, and the rationalist view which admits nothing but intellectual comprehension. It must be admitted that some theology has not escaped this kind of empiricism and this kind of rationalism.

When I speak of experience of God I will always mean pre-conceptual experience. God always transcends our senses and our intellects. We do not have access to the inner being of God. However, I will argue, this always transcending God has come close to us in love, and we can experience this presence in our lives in an obscure way. The concept of pre-conceptual experience allows us to speak of a real human awareness of God who yet remains always incomprehensible to our intellects. It is, I will argue, precisely as mystery that we experience God's presence and action.

Why Experience "of God"?

It might be helpful, at this stage, to indicate why I speak directly of experience of God, rather than using other phrases like "religious experience," "experience of grace," "Christian experience," and "mystical experience."

The problem with the expression "religious experience" is that it is not specific enough. It refers to the areas of human life where individuals and groups see themselves as related to the divine, or the sacred. Such religious experience is concerned with the relationship to the sacred which occurs through sacred rites, words, places, things and people.[8] I want to be much more specific than this. There is a need to pinpoint more precisely within general religious experience the moment of some kind of encounter with God and awareness of him.

The concept of "Christian experience," used by recent Catholic theologians,[9] is also not precise enough. Christian experience refers, according to these theologians, to the personal appropriation of the mystery of Christ within the Church. It includes participation in the Eucharist, Christian community, prayer and everyday life. However the focus of interest in this work is on one experience that may or may not occur in any of these, the sense of some kind of direct union with God. For example, where and how in the celebration of the Eucharist might a person have pre-conceptual experience of God? There is another reason for preferring "experience of God" to "Christian experience": experience of God occurs outside the Christian tradition, as well as in explicitly Christian experiences.

The phrase "experience of grace" is sometimes used by theologians to mean precisely a pre-conceptual union with God (uncreated Grace) graciously present in our lives.[10] However, the phrase is a little ambiguous, because at times writers use the word grace to mean only a created gift of God. Some who speak of "experience of grace" hold the view that we do not in any real sense have experience of God; rather we experience a created effect (created grace) which he produces in us. I want to go beyond this second position.

"Mystical experience," of course, is experience of God. But mystical experience is usually, and properly, equated with contemplative moments in prayer. Experience of God as I want to speak of it is wider than this, including both contemplative prayer and pre-conceptual experiences of God that occur because grace is poured out in our everyday lives and in our hearts. Some theologians have extended the word "mysticism" to cover our daily experience of God's grace and they speak of the "mysticism of everyday life."[11] It seems preferable, however, to speak of experience of God as a broad term with mystical experience keeping its traditional meaning as one kind of experience of God, that which occurs in contemplative prayer.

In this chapter I have been arguing that not only is it proper to speak of experience of God, but it is essential to do so if we are to be faithful to our tradition and if we are to meet the pressing pastoral needs of our times. The concept of experience has been examined and the original experiential encounter distinguished from the moment of reflective interpretation. It has been shown that experience has objective dimensions, and yet is received by a subject who must interpret it personally. Experience cannot be limited to sense experience or intellectual comprehension, but includes pre-conceptual experiences. These pre-conceptual experiences include some of the most important moments of human life, and our experience of God is always a pre-conceptual experience. Finally it has been argued that it is important to use precisely the phrase "experience of God."

The next step is to look to our human lives and ask how and where such experiences occur. The best procedure is not to describe God and then ask where we experience such a God. Rather, we must first ask where it is in human life that a person experiences moments of mystery and transcendence, and then we can draw upon the traditional, powerful word "God" and use this to speak of the one toward whom such experiences point. Then we can look to the Gospel of Jesus to illuminate our understanding of God. The beginning must be made with human experience.

two

THE MYSTERY
DIMENSION
OF OUR LIVES

For some people the word "God" carries only negative connotations. Because of unfortunate experiences in childhood the word brings to mind the picture of a harsh taskmaster, or the idea of a totally remote figure unrelated to ordinary life, or an image from religion classes of a very concrete person in the sky, a person in whom it is impossible to believe. For some people the very word "God" is so linked to negative or even boring experience that it is a blockage to a real examination of the sense of transcendence that arises in their lives. For others, of course, there is an immense and overwhelming richness in the understanding of God that comes from Christian tradition. Even this, however, is not helpful to our present task. It will be important not to pre-judge the content of what is experienced but rather to inquire about what is actually experienced.[1] Let us, then, leave aside for a short time the understanding of God that comes from Christian revelation, and the very word "God" itself, in order to see simply what is revealed in ordinary human experience. Then it will be possible to show how this experience relates to Christian revelation.

Instead of the word "God" I have chosen, along with Rahner and other theologians, to use the word "mystery." As the word is used here it does not have the meaning of a puzzle that can be solved by intelligent detective work. Rather it points to that dimension of human experience which escapes comprehension, and totally transcends us.[2]

In this chapter, I would like to examine this sense of mystery as an always-present dimension of our human experience, something that is always there in any act of knowledge or love. In the next chapter, this will be followed by a reflection on those special moments when transcendence breaks in upon our lives in a more obvious way. I will call these moments of "grace." For now we turn to the two basic human actions of knowing and loving and examine them individually, to see what can be said of a transcendent or mystery dimension in them.

The Experience of Mystery in Human Knowing

It would be possible to begin a reflection on human knowing, and on the mystery dimension of such knowing, by considering any of our everyday acts of knowledge. So we might examine our knowledge of a tree, an animal, a book or a mathematical problem. Let us, however, choose to examine the most fully human act of knowledge, our knowledge of another person.

There are two ways we might go about a reflection on our own knowing. One way is through abstract philosophical analysis.[3] The other is to invite you, the reader, to take the trouble to reflect on your own experience of knowing to see what can be discovered there. Let us take this more concrete procedure and then proceed to describe it with more exact and more abstract language. As has already been said, this exercise is not aimed at a reflection on extraordinary experiences of transcendence. The focus of attention now is on the ordinary: we are examining our own everyday knowing to see if it reveals an awareness of mystery which is always present, even if we do not notice it.

You are invited, then, to begin a reflection on your own knowing of another person. It might be helpful to choose someone with whom you are in a relationship of love. This will provide continuity with the reflection on loving that will be made in the next session.

As the person is probably not present at the time of your reflection, it is necessary to use memory and imagination to recall what occurs in your encounters with this person. In this way it is possible to recreate an act in which you know the other with precise conceptual awareness.

Call to mind the person that you know. Name the person to yourself. Notice the person's height and size, the color of hair, of skin, of eyes. Look at the contours of the person's face and the structure of forehead, cheeks, nose, mouth and jaw. It might be helpful to ask if the person seems happy and relaxed. Or is he or she anxious or tired?

Does this person work in a factory, office, business, or at home? Is he or she unemployed or a student? Does this person have close friends? Is he or she married? What do you know of the person's family? What kind of relationships does he or she enjoy?

Your knowledge of this friend of yours is much deeper than this. What are the real qualities of this person? What do you know of the person's strengths and weaknesses? What are the strong abiding concerns of your friend? What arouses feelings like anger or fear? About what does he or she care passionately? Whom does this person love?

What do you know of the heart of this person? What constitutes this person's most unique individuality?

Hold in your awareness this intellectual grasp you have of your friend. (Of course it goes without saying that this intellectual awareness does not do full justice to the other person.) It is time now to begin to examine what occurs in your consciousness as you attend, with precise conceptual knowledge, to this one person.

Notice what happens as you focus on the individual person through conceptual awareness. All your attention is given to this one person. However at the same time you single out this person with a range of concepts and judgments from other men and women. As you become conceptually aware of this one person, you also distinguish this person as concrete and individual against the world of human persons. While you are explicitly aware of this one person, there is always present an obscure awareness of all the others that this person is not.

We can go further than this. While you focus your attention in conceptual awareness on your friend, you know this person over against a background not only of all men and women, but of all beings. As you are conceptually aware of this one being (your friend) there is, at least, an obscure awareness of all the beings that this person is not. You know this particular person against the whole range of being.

An image which can help us understand this obscure awareness of the range of being is that of the horizon. A man on a journey situates a hill or a distant church spire against the horizon. He is explicitly conscious of the hill or the tower, yet he always situates it against the horizon. The horizon is there within the consciousness of the traveler as that against which everything else is seen. However, it may never become a matter of explicit concern. On the other hand the traveler may focus attention on the horizon and move toward it. Nevertheless what he grasps is only a point or points on the horizon, and he finds, as he moves toward them, that they are seen against a new horizon. The horizon itself is never quite caught.

It is possible to attend to the whole range of being that is present in consciousness as you think of one particular being, the person who is your friend. As you attend explicitly to this range of being that is backdrop and horizon for your conceptual knowledge you notice that there is no limit to this being. Your particular act of knowledge occurs against a backdrop which is without limit. As the horizon is always still beyond us when we move toward it, so this range of being escapes our attempts to exhaust it.

What our reflection reveals is that as we know this one person through conceptual awareness, we also have within our consciousness a non-explicit awareness of being without limit. Our conceptual knowledge occurs against a horizon of being which escapes limits, definitions, and our attempts to grasp it intellectually. This horizon of being without limit is what I am calling "mystery."

If this examination of our own conscious activity is put into precise language, then it is possible to say: when the human intellect reaches out to grasp another reality it does so only against a pre-conceptual awareness of being without limit. When a person knows any specific object, it is known only against a horizon of infinite mystery. This horizon is always present within the reach of consciousness, but it is not normally the focus of attention. It can, however, be attended to in the way that has just been described.

What this means, then, is that there are always two dimensions to human knowing: there is the conceptual knowledge of a specific object; there is also the pre-conceptual awareness of being without limit, of mystery.[4] The pre-conceptual awareness of mystery is actually the condition for our conceptual knowledge of a concrete person, or being.

The Experience of the Mystery of Love in Human Loving

We have examined our knowledge of another person and found that in this knowing of a particular individual we already have a non-explicit and obscure awareness of being without limits. We know conceptually against a horizon of infinite mystery. Let us turn now to a reflection on our own loving in order to see what this reveals.[5]

It will be helpful, then, to recreate a moment of love for a person in your life through the use of your own memory and imagination. What you need to do is catch yourself loving another so that you can explore the dimensions of your loving which do not always receive full attention.

As you recreate a free act of loving it is important to begin to notice the range of such love. Is it not true that such love reaches out beyond this one person to include others? Does not your love for this one person also include a dimension of good will to other men and women? Perhaps we can go further than this. People who are "in love" find that the whole of life changes. Colors seem richer, nature comes alive in new and unexpected ways. The love between two people somehow embraces more than the individuals, more even than other men and women in their lives. It includes an opening of the person to the whole of reality.

In your love for this one person, is there not an opening out in trusting love which embraces all? Is it not true that there is an element in your love which moves toward the infinite mystery which surrounds your life and your love?

Let us move from an examination of the range of your love to consider the sense of gift which accompanies love. Does not the other person appear as somebody that is given to you? Is he or she not experienced as more than you can possibly account for? Is not the very bond of love that joins you experienced as something more than can be accounted for by the two people involved? Is not the union of love experienced as a mysterious gift? When you begin to reflect upon yourself loving, and all that this involves in terms of self-forgetfulness, forgiveness, fidelity, is there not always a sense that your own love for another is mysterious and somehow given to you?

Simple reflection on our own loving reveals that it has a dimension which reaches out beyond the other person to include the whole mystery of what is. At the same time in our love we know that all is somehow given to us. Our love embraces even the mystery that surrounds our lives, and we experience our love as given to us in mystery.

Reflection on our knowing reveals that whenever we have conceptual knowledge of another person we also experience being without limit in a pre-conceptual, mysterious way. Reflection on our love of another person reveals that our love is given to us mysteriously and reaches out to embrace all of reality, even the mystery that always surrounds our human existence. What we experience, then in our conceptual knowledge and love of concrete finite beings is a pre-conceptual awareness of being without limit and an opening out of ourselves in trusting love toward the whole of life. The mystery that surrounds our existence presents itself to us both as the ground of our knowledge and love and also as that toward which they strive. We have taken as our starting point our own experience of other persons and discovered that it is always accompanied by a sense of mystery, a pre-conceptual awareness of being without limits.

The Other Person, the Self and Mystery

The reflection on the transcendent dimension of our knowing and loving of another person suggests certain conclusions to us. It shows, first of all, that our encounter with mystery occurs in life through our encounter with specific objects (in this case, another person) in our world. Our awareness of being without limit occurs when we go out of ourselves in knowledge of another, and the sense of a love beyond ourselves occurs in the very act of our human loving.

What this suggests is that our experience of mystery depends upon and occurs in our experience of the daily reality in our world. We have examined the high point of our everyday experience, our knowledge and love of other persons. It would have been possible to reflect upon our knowledge of any particular object and to show that such conceptual knowledge depends upon a co-present sense of mystery, of being without limits. However we have focused on our knowledge and love of another person, because this is the high point of our human conscious life, and because it is precisely here that we have the richest awareness of the mystery of love in our lives.

The experience of mystery arises only in our experience of actual events in our lives. The experience of mystery depends upon our encounter with our world. However in one particular encounter, our meeting with another human being, we experience mystery as the horizon and ground for what is most personal and most human. In our love of others we discover a dimension of love which encompasses the whole of reality and leads us again into mystery. It can be said, then, that the experience of mystery occurs in the movement out from self and that it occurs in its most human and personal form in our relationships with other persons. Experience of mystery occurs in social relationships.[6] The core of our religious sense occurs in and through society. This truth will be returned to later in our discussion of the social and historical dimensions of our experience of God.

For now it is enough to stress that we encounter mystery in and through the day to day encounters with our world. This experience arises in and through our own specific history, and it arises in and through our social relationships.

On the other hand we can turn this around and say that we can know our neighbor only against the horizon of infinite being. All our knowledge of specific persons or things in our world depends upon an awareness of being without limits. This awareness of mystery may not be made explicit in our consciousness, but it must be there. It is the condition for our conceptual knowledge of any one thing or any one person. And when we love another person we know that love depends upon a love already given in life and reaches beyond this one person to all of what is.

The two experiences, then, go together in our lives. We experience mystery originally only in our encounter with specific persons or things in our everyday world. Our experience of mystery depends upon our everyday knowledge and love. On the other hand we know and love only in the light of this horizon of loving mystery in our lives. The two experiences are necessarily linked together and depend upon each other.

However there is another element in this that we have not so far examined in any detail. This is our sense of ourselves. How do we become aware of our own individuality? The answer to this has to be that we truly know ourselves only as we encounter other beings in our world and distinguish ourselves from them. Again, the highest moment in this will be our encounter with other persons. In our experience of other men and women we necessarily distinguish them from ourselves. We may not be explicitly conscious of ourselves; the focus of our attention may be the other person. Nevertheless to experience the other, there must be present in our consciousness at least a non-explicit and general awareness of our own selves as distinct from the others.

Most of us would affirm the truth of this from a very general reflection on the pattern of our lives. We know how much our sense of ourselves has grown through the individual relationships of our lives.

However, our sense of ourselves as different from the other person also depends upon our ability to situate ourselves and the other against the backdrop of being without limits. Just as we can reflect about our knowing of another person and find that we can only know this person against the horizon of being without limits, so too a little reflection shows that we can only come to know ourselves against such a horizon. When we know ourselves as distinct from another person, we necessarily situate ourselves and the other person against this background. Our experience of ourselves occurs only against the horizon of mystery.[7]

We can confirm that our knowledge of ourselves is dependent upon an experience of infinite mystery by a general reflection on our own lives. The times when we have the deepest sense of ourselves are times when life is filled with mystery and often with a kind of awe and a deep sense of gratitude. Since we will be exploring some of these experiences in our next chapter there is no need to pursue the matter here.

What has been suggested here is that there are three experiences which always and necessarily occur together—our experience of another, our experience of ourselves and our experience of infinite mystery. Each depends upon the other two. All are present within consciousness, although we may be explicitly attending only to the other person who is the object of our knowledge and love.

As we come to the end of this section it might be well to point to the limits of what can be claimed as a result of the kind of reflection we have been doing. We have found that in our knowledge and love there is an experience of an horizon of being that is without limit. At the heart of our ordinary human activity is the experience of mystery. However, we cannot give this mystery a positive content.[8] We cannot describe for ourselves an infinite being whom we experience. All that we can say is that what we experience cannot be limited, that it moves into infinity. We discover in ourselves a dynamism toward the infinite, but the term of this movement cannot be grasped. It remains mysterious.[9]

The kind of reflection that we are undertaking here is, of course, but one way of attempting to describe the way in which we human beings come to some awareness of God in our lives. There are many other approaches to this question, such as the illumination theory of Augustine, the second-level deductive approach of Aquinas and some contemporary theology,[10] and the knowledge-through-love approach of the mystics.[11] However the transcendental approach taken here is, it seems to me, a more immediate and helpful way of opening up the question for many men and women today.

three

EXPERIENCE OF GRACE

A farmer who had agreed, reluctantly, to attend a workshop on Christian faith found himself confronted with the question: "Is there any special time in your life when you find yourself overwhelmed by a sense that there is something more than yourself involved, something more than you can account for, a time when something seems like a gift given from beyond yourself?" For the first time, in a session lasting several hours, the farmer's face showed interest, and after a while he volunteered a comment: "I feel like that sometimes in the early mornings when I am out in the middle of a crop of wheat and I hold a grain of new wheat in my hand." He went on to say that he had never talked to anyone about this experience before, even though it had happened over many years. The experience had been so overwhelming as to be almost inexpressible, and he had felt that others would not understand what he was talking about. As the discussion continued it became clear that, while the farmer went to church regularly, and sometimes prayed, he had never, to this point, explicitly connected his experience in his wheat crop with anything in his Christian faith.

In this chapter I would like to move beyond the consideration of the always-present but seldom-noticed experience of mystery that was dealt with in the last chapter in order to focus on experiences like that of the farmer. It will be helpful to explore some of those moments in our lives when something beyond ourselves breaks in upon our awareness in a noticeable way. Such experiences of transcendence I will call moments of "grace."

The traditional word "grace" carries with it connotations of something which comes upon us in surprising and mysterious ways. It refers to something which comes to us as a free gift, beyond our expectations or hopes. I would like to use the word in this way, for the time being, without giving it the full weight that it can carry in Christian theology. Later it will be important to explore, in the light of the Gospel, something of the theological nature of the experience of grace. For now it will be helpful to restrict ourselves to a description of what can be claimed simply on the basis of experience. Experience of grace, then, is the experience of something which transcends us, which breaks in upon our day to day existence in a mysterious way, and which we experience as a gift given to us.

Are there such experiences in our lives? Are there times when something mysterious occurs in day to day activity so that we find ourselves open to a world beyond the everyday? Are there times in life where we have a sense that there is more to this particular experience than we can account for? Are there times when we have a sense that we are given this moment, this person, this experience?

What is needed then is a description of the kinds of moments when a sense of mystery or of transcendence invades our lives.[1] This description will open out into a theological approach to the experience of God, as these human experiences are brought into dialogue with the Gospels and the tradition in the chapters that follow.

Any attempt to describe and evoke such experiences of grace is bound to be a little arbitrary. These kinds of experiences are very personal, and such moments occur in vastly different ways in the lives of different people. Yet it seems to me that there are some basic ways in which men and women encounter transcendence in their lives, even if they never describe it as such. I would argue that such experiences can be broadly classified into two groups: they are either positive experiences pointing to a fullness and a richness beyond the person involved, or they are negative experiences of limitation. The experience of grace always occurs in limit situations, when our small, secure world comes apart and we are open to mystery; even the positive experiences include a negative point where we recognize that what is given transcends ourselves and our capacity for comprehension.

Experience of Grace in the Richness of Life

There are five experiences (interpersonal love, childbirth, creativity, forgiveness and beauty of the world) that are arbitrarily singled out in the pages that follow as moments when we may be taken by a sense of excessive richness, of superabundance, and the awareness that "all is given" and that what is given cannot be attributed to ourselves.

Interpersonal Love

The experience which most obviously brings with it the awareness that all is gift is the encounter of love between two people. The last chapter included a reflection upon the process of love itself which pointed toward the sense of mystery that always accompanies such loving. However, this always present, but hidden, sense of mystery, is not our concern right now. The focus now is on more obvious experiences of richness, where a particular moment of union with another positively leads to a sense of transcendence and grace at the heart of the experience.

Men and women who have learned to love each other in married life experience that all is gift in their love for their partners. The experience of grace occurs at the heart of their relationship. Some will point to early ecstatic moments when loving and being loved was an overwhelming joy. Some point to the moments of sexual union, times of passionate abandonment and radical trust. Others remember times of struggle where maturing love coped with doubts, with failure and with the pain of life, and still endured, seemingly freer and richer than before.

The experience of grace at the core of our relationships is not hard for us to find and name. Young couples preparing for marriage, if asked whether they experience their partner as given to them, as a free gift that they in no way deserve, and whether their mutual love is not itself a most amazing and unaccountable gift, will often answer with a strong "Yes!" with a sense of gratitude that this mystery has been articulated.

This experience of grace occurs not only in the powerful and dramatic experiences of union between man and woman, but in the simpler experiences of friendship, in the peace and joy that comes from being with old friends, in the confidence that the other can cope with our own inadequacy, in the sense of trust in our friend that does not have limits. In these and many other ways, our deep relationships open up onto the world of mystery and we know that all is given to us.

Even a brief encounter with another person can open out into the world of mystery when we glimpse something in the other which takes us beyond the vision of the other as an object, to some kind of contact with the depths of this human person before us.

Childbirth

Perhaps there is no more profound sense of a gift than that which occurs in a person in the birth of his or her own child. For many, at such a time, there is an overwhelming sense of the mystery of life.

There is no doubt that most parents today have access to

enough science to be able to account for the conception, gestation and birth of a child. Much of the ignorance of earlier times has been replaced by a biological understanding which can make sense of the whole process. Yet parents who know all of this, and who certainly know that the child is the product of their own bodies, still find themselves overwhelmed by the mystery of the child they hold. They sense that they are co-creators of this child with something that is beyond them.

A child that is the product of the love of two people is still received by them as a miracle. For many, childbirth is a time when they know the experience of grace in its purest form.

As a child grows and his or her personality develops and matures, there develops the wonder that precisely this child, this unique individual, has been given to its parents. Those who adopt children often speak of their own special moments of wonder at the mystery of this particular child whose life has been linked with their own.

Creativity

A third kind of experience in which we may have a sense of mystery and of grace is in the moment of creativity that occurs in each of our lives. Poets have traditionally accredited their inspiration to something outside themselves and their own skills with words. They stand in need of something that is breathed in by the poetic muse. When the muse is absent no amount of work seems to bear fruit. At other times the work flows and the writer knows that inspiration has somehow been given.

All of us know this sense of creativity in different ways—in writing letters, in gardening, in arranging a room, a table or a bowl of flowers, in a whole range of crafts. Many of us would remember the first time we created something in a particular medium, perhaps the first time we worked with clay and made a clumsy pot. In the process we may have touched something that emerges from deep within and felt a sense of being in tune with the mystery of our own being, and with the mystery of life that transcends us. It is precisely when our own depths are touched that we are likely to have the sense that we are mysteries to ourselves and cannot adequately account for what we produce.

Forgiveness

Another of the experiences in which we know the sense of grace is the moment when, for no reason that we can account for, our hearts are freed to move beyond their hardened boundaries. One of the best examples of this is the moment of forgiveness. Often we feel trapped in a world of anger and bitterness because of the words or actions of another. Sometimes there is a whole "logic" which supports our own position. We feel that it would be doing a disservice to truth or justice for us to give in to the other. Our hardness of heart is reinforced by a whole series of rational arguments.

Then for no obvious reason, we are drawn to reach out to the other person in a free, forgiving, word or action. Suddenly our own hearts are softened and our eyes are opened and we see the other person and his or her position. We are able to walk in the shoes of the other person and can look back amazed at our own former position. Such everyday conversions we know as experiences of grace.

It happens in another way when we meet someone when we are weary and inattentive, and the other person does not appeal to us at all, and we tend to be absent even as we speak with him or her. Then something happens that reveals the true humanity of the other. We experience this as a movement of our own hearts in which we really meet this person before us. Then for the first time we begin to see the person as the overwhelming mystery he or she is. Again, we must name this an experience of grace.

The Beauty of Nature

Finally there is the experience we have when we notice something in the world around us, and suddenly, perhaps for the first time, we really see what is before us. We might be out walking, when, for example, we notice the range of colors before us as sunlight is filtered through the leaves of trees.

For each of us there are special times and places which bring us the experience of extraordinary peace and the sense of being in tune with a world beyond ourselves. There are other times when nature looms before us as immense and powerful, and we know how small we are before these mysterious forces. We all respond differently, but most of us would admit that there is something in nature that opens up to the sense of mystery.

There is the perfection of a single flower that can captivate us, the depths of space at night, lit by stars which entrance us with their loveliness and whose number and size dazzle our minds, the sunrise and sunset which fill our skies with extravagant color and set the rhythm of our days.

These kinds of experiences can be truly moments of grace. They touch us deeply and the human heart spontaneously lifts in thanksgiving. At times like these we can experience a human need to offer praise.

Experience of Grace in Limit Situations

The experiences that we have been reflecting upon are all positive. They become experiences of grace precisely because in them we know ourselves as unaccountably blessed. They are moments filled with richness, a richness which exceeds our hopes and expectations, which pushes us to acknowledge that all is given to us. In these experiences there is an implicit negative moment: the recognition that we are limited and the gift given transcends our limits. Something is given and it comes from what is beyond us.

There are other situations which are, at least in the first instance, primarily negative. In them we come up against our limits and yet in this very confrontation are taken beyond ourselves into the mystery of grace. Among these moments are the experiences of vulnerability, of death, of failure, of loneliness and of alienation.

Vulnerability

Vulnerability is so linked to our sense of what it is to be human that we are inclined to say that those who are not vulnerable are somehow inhuman. We find ourselves easily identifying with people who experience their own vulnerability, and often those who appear strong and impervious to life's dangers are difficult for us to relate with. They appear to us as superhuman or as men and women who are hiding from their true humanity.

In fact, most of us would admit that we are often guilty of masking our own vulnerability, and of running away from it. We do this in many ways—by throwing all our energies into work so that there is no space left for unsettling experience of our own fragile grasp on existence, by filling in the space in our life by constant social activity, by entertainment which reduces us to non-thinking passivity. Even the time before sleep is sometimes effectively nullified through alcohol or other drugs.

Facing up to our vulnerability appears as a dangerous task. The experience that we are contingent, that we have no real right to be, but are dependent for our existence on another, frightens us. We begin to know that of ourselves we are without meaning and without direction. We cannot account for our beginning or our future. We know that we have a fragile grasp even on our own identity. Who are we really when the props that we use to give meaning begin to fall away? There are times when we know that the props do fall, and that our final meaning is not given by the love of others or by our work. All things pass.

When we allow ourselves to be touched by this truth of our lives, when we know our own vulnerability instead of running from it, we can experience our radical dependence on the gracious mystery that upholds us. Such moments of poverty and trust can be deep experiences of grace.

Death

Death, and the threat of death, is the ultimate limit that faces each of us. Moments when we confront death, especially the death of someone who is spouse, child, parent or friend to us, can be the darkest hours of our existence. We can feel that there is absolutely nothing left and all is dark and meaningless.

Yet when men and women look back on the pattern of their days they will point to such times as moments when they knew a sense of mystery and of grace in their lives. They report that over the weeks and months and years of mourning there developed a sense of being upheld and supported in their sorrow. Even in the loss, there was a sense of presence that led to peace. Hopelessness gave way to hope, and the conviction of a future union with the loved person grew clearer.

The great religious traditions have always known that confrontation with death is intimately connected with experience of God. For this reason the Buddhist monk has been required to spend all night meditating in a cemetery, and the Christian mystics have often been pictured with skulls as part of their room decoration. We might well prefer to avoid these practices but we cannot avoid the day to day confrontations with death. These provide the ground for that final act of trust in which we hand ourselves over into mystery.

Failure

A third limit situation is that of failure. How often we unconsciously presume that religious experience is naturally linked with success! As has already been suggested we can and do experience grace in the joy of creativity and accomplishment. The Gospels report Jesus' joy at the disciples' successful ministry, and this leads immediately to a beautiful prayer of praise and wonder (Lk 10:21). However the major pattern in the life of Jesus is failure. His mission fails, his friends fail him, he dies an outcast and a failure.

Failure forces us to confront our finite condition. Perhaps this is particularly true when our failed project is something we had presumed was "of God." We are suddenly confronted with the possibility that our plans and hopes are not the last word to be spoken on the matter. We are forced into a much bigger world, and are again called to know our own self-centeredness, and to surrender again into mystery. Such acceptance of personal failure in our projects, in hope and trust that all can be brought unto good, is truly experience of grace.

Even the willful failure that is personal sin can be a time of forgiveness and grace. Even when we know deeply the sin of our world and our own part in it, we can turn to the source of life in radical trust. This is the experience that Julian of Norwich records. Her Lord tells her: "It is true that sin is the cause of all this pain, but all shall be well, and all shall be well, and all manner of things shall be well."[2]

Loneliness

Loneliness is also closely connected with our sense of vulnerability and with our fear of death. It is so common an experience that it hardly needs description. Somctimes it seems that the deeper the love in our lives the more empty are the times when we are alone.

Yet loneliness can be life-giving. It can become something from which we refuse to run and, instead, something which we embrace. When loneliness is accepted and not run from, it can become solitude, a place where we encounter the mystery of ourselves and the mystery that is beyond us.[3] Solitude is a time where we come to know ourselves before a silent presence which transcends us. There is an acceptance and a peace that comes from recognizing that finally we cannot escape our solitude.

We have the choice in our lives between a lifelong flight from loneliness, which runs the grave risk of manipulating other persons into the impossible position of attempting to meet the infinite need in us, and the acceptance of a life in which solitude and companionship both have a part. It might be said that we can only love freely once we have learned to enter into solitude and to accept it. Solitude teaches us that another person cannot be God for us. In acceptance of solitude we learn the limits of human love and come to know that it cannot exhaust our need for love, and must not pretend to do so. Here we can find freedom to deal with our possessiveness and dependency, and we may learn the ability to relate to others in a way which respects freedom and differences.

When loneliness becomes solitude, then it is truly an experience of grace.

Alienation

Finally, we experience alienation. We feel out of touch with the whole of our world and nothing has meaning. Perhaps there is rupture between ourselves and those we love; perhaps we experience rupture within our own person. The beauty of our world means nothing. Such moments can leave us with a sense that there is nothing left. No created person or thing gives consolation. Then perhaps we can still reach out into the darkness that surrounds us and call out in trust. There is nowhere else to go.

The experience of alienation can be totally destructive of a person. It can cripple. Yet it can also become a moment of grace. I think, in this context, of men and women who endure the pain of a marriage that has failed, yet struggle on living their lives as best they can, and come to find strength and peace in their lives. Some of these will say that they have rediscovered the love of God in a whole new way, in and through the rupture of the most important relationship in their lives.

These experiences, of richness and of limitation, are but a few examples of the many ways in which moments of grace occur in our lives. However such experience cannot be confined to any set of categories. Grace breaks through in each life in a way that is unique for each individual. However the attempt to articulate some of the ways in which we experience grace is useful if it helps a person to look to his or her own life and notice what is given there.

So far we have discussed two basic ways in which we may experience ourselves as related to what is beyond us: the first is the experience of mystery which accompanies our ordinary knowing and loving; the second is the experience of grace and transcendence which breaks in upon our lives at certain times. At this stage all that has been attempted is an evocation of these experiences, the attempt to bring them to consciousness and to describe them. The next step in the process will be an inquiry into the nature of these experiences. To do this we will need to appeal to the Christian tradition. It is in Jesus Christ that we find the answers to the questions raised by the abiding mystery in our lives and the experience of moments of grace. We need, now, to go beyond a reflection on what we actually experience to find our experience illuminated by the Gospel of Jesus.

four

JESUS AND THE EXPERIENCE OF GOD

Someone who has followed the argument of this book so far might well say: "Yes, I do have some abiding sense of mystery in my life, of something at the core of my own person that is beyond my comprehension; and I can agree that there are moments in my life when I find myself invaded by a sense of presence, when life seems given to me as a free gift; but what do these experiences have to do with the Christian God I learned about as a child?" It is one thing to become aware of transcendence in our lives. It is quite another to talk about "experience of God." What is the connection between the experiences of mystery and grace discussed in the last two chapters and the Christian God?

This chapter is aimed at bringing the experience of transcendence into dialogue with the Christian Gospel concerning God. The Christian Gospel is best seen, it seems to me, as an answer to the question raised by the experience of transcendence in our lives. There is no way of proving, in an absolute way, that it is *the* answer. The Christian Gospel does claim to be the final and definitive answer, but if a person is to accept it as such, then he or she can only embrace it in a movement of faith. Only an individual can say for himself or herself; "Yes, this God of Jesus is that for which my whole being hungers. I will stake my life on this."

Before examining the Christian message about God it will be helpful to connect the word "God" with the human experience of transcendence and mystery. This word can now be introduced into the discussion to describe the mysterious origin and goal of the human experience of transcendence. When a woman becomes aware of mystery at the heart of her knowing and loving, then she can legitimately use the word "God" to describe that toward which her own experience of mystery points. When a man experiences something in his life as a moment of grace, for which he can in no way give an account, then he can use the word "God" to describe the mysterious origin of this gift. This is not to pre-judge the issue of the nature of the origin and goal of mystery in our lives, but simply, at this stage, to give it a name.

We experience moments of transcendence and grace which open up toward something beyond us. We experience a movement into mystery at the heart of our humanity. The goal of this movement can be called "God" as long as it is recognized that not much can be said about this "God" on the basis of the kind of reflection we have been doing.

It would be dishonest to give the word "God" the meaning that it carries in the Christian tradition, or in the great religions of the world, and then to pretend that it has been established that such a God exists. All that we have established is that there is an experience of mystery and transcendence which occurs at the center of human life. If we call the goal of this mystery "God" then this is legitimate as long as we acknowledge the limits of what we can establish about this "God" from our reflection on our own experience. As has been already said it is important to notice how little we can claim to know about this "God" as a result of our reflections.

The following observations attempt to summarize what can be said about that to which our experience of transcendence points: the experience of mystery points to what is without limits; it occurs as the very ground of our human knowing and loving; there are times when transcendence breaks in upon our lives in bounteous and graceful ways; this mystery appears as the hidden origin and goal of our loving; it occurs at the heart of what is most personal and most human; we experience a radical dependency on this mystery. We cannot claim much more than this as a result of a reflection on what we experience. If we call "God" that to which our experience of mystery points, then this is all that can be said about such a God.

The human heart, however, hungers for much more than this. To what extent is this God a personal God? Is God distant and unavailable to us or close and seeking relationship with us? Do we stand before this God as despicable and guilty or as forgiven and free? Is this God in a world above us or involved in our human history? Is this God a God of the rich and powerful or a God of the poor? These and many other questions cannot be answered in a simple reflection on our experience.

There is, however, an answer given in Jesus Christ. It is this answer that needs exploration at this point. It is time now to turn to the Christian Gospels to see how they illuminate this human experience of mystery. It is important to again note, however, that there can be no compelling proof that will force a person to leap from his or her own experience of mystery toward faith in Jesus and the God that he reveals. All that theology can do is to point the way from experience of mystery to the Gospel interpretation of this mystery, and to show the lines of relationship between the two.

Jesus' Experience of God as Abba

Jesus' own experience of God is, I will argue, reflected in two expressions that have profound significance for him:

"Abba" and "kingdom of God." These two expressions can be seen as the key objective interpretations in language of Jesus' own encounter with the mystery of God in his life.

The Gospels give us no direct insight into the inner life of Jesus or into his own encounters with God, and our knowledge of Jesus' own experience is limited to what we know from the New Testament. However a critical approach to the New Testament does reveal some crucial information about Jesus' encounters with God.

The basic Gospel structure suggests certain important things about Jesus' own religious experience. The Synoptic Gospels present Jesus' baptism in the Jordan River as a central moment in his life. Here he has an extraordinary experience of the Holy Spirit and comes to a sense of his unique sonship and mission. From that moment he is "led by the Spirit" in his life and the Spirit leads him first to the solitude of the desert. Jesus returns from the desert to preach that the reign of God is imminent and, in some way, breaking in on the world. The response to the coming of God's reign must be conversion. In his meals, his healing, his forgiveness and his association with outcasts Jesus announces the reign of God by way of action. He mediates this reign of God in word; his parables reveal the mystery of God at the heart of all reality.

Who is God for Jesus? What kind of experience of God lies behind his preaching and practice of the kingdom? Central to the answer to these questions is the name that Jesus gives to God: his God is Abba. Critical biblical scholarship sees the Gospels as heavily influenced by the post-Easter activity of the early Church. It is suspicious about loose claims about what can be attributed directly to the historical Jesus. However there is no doubt at all among biblical scholars that Jesus himself used the word "Abba" as a name for God.[1]

Jesus constantly addresses God as "Father" in the Gospels, often as "my Father." However in St. Mark's account of the agony in the garden we find the words: "And he said, 'Abba, Father, all things are possible to thee; remove this cup from me; yet not what I will, but what thou wilt' " (Mk 14:36). Mark has preserved the ancient Aramaic word "Abba" that is translated into Greek, and now into English, as Father. This suggests the possibility that Abba may lie behind the other New Testament passages where Jesus speaks to the Father. In fact this is the conclusion of scholars like Joachim Jeremias. Jeremias has studied the question intensively and he argues that an Abba lies behind every instance where the New Testament speaks of Jesus' prayer to the Father.[2]

From the Letters of Paul we learn that the use of the word "Abba" was widespread in the early Church. Writing to the church he had founded at Galatia Paul declares: "And because you are sons, God has sent the Spirit of his Son into our hearts, crying, 'Abba! Father' " (4:6). Then in the heart of his Letter to the Christians at Rome, a community he had not visited, Paul writes: "When we cry, 'Abba! Father!' it is the Spirit himself bearing witness with our spirit that we are children of God" (8:15–16). Clearly, there was a widespread practice in the early Church of using Jesus' name for God. Paul simply assumes familiarity with this style of prayer in the churches he was addressing whether founded by himself or not. For Paul, to be given Jesus' own name for God is to share Jesus' own relationship with the Father. We are adopted children and can use the name, because of the Spirit present in our hearts.

This word "Abba," then, is the key word in Jesus' own experience of God, and in his mediation of that experience to his disciples. It is important to explore its content a little more. It has already been said that Jesus seems always to address God as Abba. It is striking that Jesus' Jewish contemporaries never address God as Abba. There is reason for this. The word was originally simply a baby's word for father, a word like "Papa" or "Daddy." It was one of the first words a child would utter. At the time of Jesus the word was used by adults of their own fathers.[3] However, such a word was not used of God, for the same reason, perhaps, that many people today would be slow to address God as "Daddy": it seems to imply a kind of disrespectful familiarity.

Jesus' use of this word is unique and individual. It expresses the heart of his own encounter with God. It speaks of intimacy and familiarity, of boundless confidence and childlike trust. It speaks also of uncompromising obedience, an obedience that would lead to the cross. Jesus' unique sense of his own sonship and of his own mission is tied to his experience of God as Abba.

Like us, Jesus lived his life from day to day, and in the ordinary events of life he too has a sense of the infinite mystery surrounding human life. He gives himself to this mystery in love, knows it in the hours and nights of prayer and in the day to day struggles of life. He dares to reach out into the darkness and mystery which he has come to know as love and to call the mystery "Abba." His prayer is nourished and fostered by the long history of spirituality in Israel, but this tradition is concentrated in Jesus in his own unique Abba experience.

Edward Schillebeeckx has said that Jesus' original Abba experience is "source and secret of his being, message and manner of life."[4] Everything depends upon this experience and everything is shaped by it.

The Abba experience is the source and foundation for Jesus' words and deeds, his attempt to live each moment in trusting fidelity to the Father's will and his free acceptance of the confrontation and struggle that leads to his death.

This experience, then, is not an isolated prayer experience with no impact on everyday life and history. There will be reason to explore this matter more fully when Jesus' concept of the kingdom of God is examined. For now, it can be insisted that the New Testament reveals that the experience of God as Abba is the experience of a God who is totally on the side of men and women, a God whose passion is human well-being, a God who is active saving love.

Schillebeeckx writes: "Jesus' Abba experience is an immediate awareness of God as a power cherishing people and making them free."[5] The experience of God as Abba impels Jesus, and his disciples, toward the love of other men and women who are, then, one's brothers and sisters. Furthermore since God is Abba it is the poorest and the weakest that are his special love. This God of Jesus, this Abba, is the God of the little people, the God of the poor, the God of sinners, the God of the lost sheep. Because God is Abba, he is loved when we love our brothers and sisters. This, of course, means a radical deepening of the old law and a whole new freedom, which is precisely what we find in the life and ministry of Jesus.

Jesus' ministry of healing and forgiveness, his stance with the poorest and with the sinners, his confrontation with those who teach a harsh and unbending God of law, his announcing of the good news of the kingdom, must all be seen as directly related to his experience of God. The Abba experience is the central driving force in the life of Jesus and it is what enables him to surrender in trust to the darkness of death.

The Reign of God

There can only be one answer to the question: What is the primary concern of Jesus of Nazareth? His whole life is built around one central reality: the kingdom of God, God's active reign.[6]

Jesus not only preaches the kingdom, he acts it out. He announces and celebrates the kingdom in his own deeds. As he gathers disciples, heals the sick and forgives sin, his actions announce the coming of God's kingdom. As he eats with outcasts and sinners he celebrates in anticipation the feast of the kingdom. When he confronts those who imprison God within human laws, he does this in the name of God and his active will to bring life and salvation.

Finally, it is out of fidelity to God's active reign in his own life that Jesus accepts his own death. The kingdom is the unifying theme that gives meaning to the whole life and to the death of Jesus of Nazareth.

There can be no doubt that Jesus sees, in his own life and ministry, signs that the final eschatological action of God has begun. In his own words and deeds the long-awaited moment has arrived and the Spirit of God is at last being poured out upon a suffering world. In Luke's Gospel Jesus is portrayed as quoting Isaiah 61 in the synagogue at Nazareth:

> The Spirit of the Lord is upon me,
> because he has anointed me
> to preach good news to the poor.
> He has sent me to proclaim release to the captives
> and recovering of sight to the blind
> to set at liberty those who are oppressed,
> to proclaim the acceptable year of the Lord (4:18–19).

When John's disciples are sent to ask Jesus whether he is the one they had been waiting for, he simply asks them to look and listen to the way God's power is evident in his own ministry (Mt 11:2–6; Lk 7:18–23). Again he refers to Isaiah 61: the sick are healed and the poor have the good news preached to them. These texts, no doubt, owe something to the creative activity of the post-Easter Church and the Gospel writers. However their central insight, that Jesus sees the eschatological Spirit of God at work in his own ministry, cannot be denied.

Nothing is more certain about the historical Jesus than his

healing of those afflicted with evil spirits. This activity provokes the shocking accusation from his enemies that he exorcises demons by the power of Beelzebub; Jesus responds with the saying; "But if it is by the Spirit of God that I cast out demons, then the kingdom of God has come upon you" (Mt 12:28). This saying, which seems certainly to go back to the historical Jesus, is recorded also by Luke (11:20) where Jesus speaks of the "finger of God" rather than the "Spirit of God." The finger of God is an Old Testament (Ex 8:19) way of speaking of God's power, or his Spirit. The presence of the power of the Spirit in Jesus' ministry manifests the presence of God's reign.

Jesus was conscious of the presence of the eschatological Spirit in his own words and deeds. This is the sure sign of the coming of the kingdom of God. Jesus' experience of God is, then, twofold: he experiences God as Abba, and he experiences God as Spirit, and as power, in his own ministry. James Dunn has put this well: "Jesus thought of himself as God's Son and as anointed by the eschatological Spirit, because in prayer he experienced God as Father and in ministry he experienced a power to heal which he could only understand as the power of the end-time and an inspiration to proclaim a message which he could only understand as the Gospel of the end-time."[7]

The kingdom of God is at the heart of the preaching of Jesus. He announces that God is breaking in on our world, turning our small securities upside down, and calling us to radical conversion and a whole new way of life.[8] The parables show that this in-breaking of God, which will come in our future, has already begun. The mystery of this event can be seen in the reality of everyday life for those who have eyes to see and ears to hear. The kingdom is present in the ordinary, but hidden like a tiny mustard seed, like fine yeast, whose smallness and hiddenness belie the power and the energy and the life that will one day be revealed.

Jesus does not preach about himself. However, we must also say that he does not simply preach about God. He preaches the Kingdom of God and lives his life in accordance with this kingdom. What he announces in word and deed is always God in relationship, God with men and women, God in action, a God "on the side of" humanity.[9] Jesus' God is always a God concerned and active about the well-being of men and women and their relationship with one another. This God is one who saves, a God whose passion is to bring health and wholeness to humanity. The message of liberation is at the heart of the preaching and the practice of the kingdom of God. The God whom Jesus experiences as Abba is a God of the oppressed and the poor, one who has their well-being at heart.

The God of Jesus can never be made irrelevant to the realities of human suffering, to evil. When there is slavery, oppression and exploitation this God can never be invoked to sanction what exists. Where this is attempted (and it often is) it is in total contradiction to Jesus' experience of God and his preaching of the liberating and saving reign of God, and the kind of radical conversion that this calls for in men and women.[10]

If we preserve Jesus' own images of God, "Abba" and "God reigning," then our Christianity will avoid the always present danger of being simply another religion which places flowers on the chains that bind people. Jesus' God calls us to confront the real suffering of our brothers and sisters and to break the chains.

It is impossible to attempt to synthesize the meaning of "kingdom" for Jesus here. The word is, after all, a powerful symbol whose richness is inexhaustible.[11] It points to the incomprehensible mystery of God. The symbol "kingdom of God" can only be given its proper content through a thorough study of the words and deeds of Jesus. Such a study is beyond the scope of this discussion.

What can be said, however, is that Jesus' experience of God finds expression in his language, as "Abba" and as "kingdom of God." A brief study of those expressions, and the meaning given them by Jesus' words and deeds, has shown us something of the God that Jesus experiences.

The New Testament, then, offers an answer to the earlier questions about the God we experience in our own lives. This God, the Gospel tells us, is not distant and aloof but one who comes close to us in compassion and warmth. The God of Jesus surrounds us with love and constantly invites us into relationship. This Abba does not hold our sins against us, but offers unconditional forgiveness and inner healing. This is not a God who can be invoked to support the rich and the powerful in their exploitation of their brothers and sisters. This God is a God of all men and women, but one who is in a special way the God of the poorest. Such a God is not remote from our human history; rather he is one who is always involved, always active to save, always challenging and inviting us to the task of full human liberation.

Obviously these answers could be developed by a closer study of the Gospels. But perhaps enough has been mentioned here to show the direction of the revelation that is given in the words which Jesus puts around his own experiences of God.

Jesus—Word of God and Way to the Father

We have been reflecting on Jesus' own experience of God, as Abba and as God reigning, and exploring something of what Jesus reveals about the mystery that encompasses our lives. To entrust ourselves to this mystery in love and to name it Abba, and to build our lives upon this kingdom of God, is to place our faith in this Jesus and what he reveals. Our faith in this God of

Jesus, our faith that God is indeed Abba to us, is built upon faith in Jesus.

The disciples of Jesus, in the light of the resurrection, were able to make this act of faith. They were able to go further: not only did they come to see that Jesus reveals the Father to us, but they came to understand the meaning of what Jesus says in John's Gospel: "I and the Father are one," and "To see me is to see the Father." This insight of faith was given classic formulation in the Council of Chalcedon of 541. This Council declared that in the one person Jesus Christ there are two natures: "Our Lord Jesus Christ is one and the same Son, the same perfect in Godhead, the same perfect in manhood, truly God and truly man. . . ."

The full meaning of this affirmation cannot be explored here, but it is important to reflect briefly about what it means in terms of our interest in the human experience of God. On the one hand, since Jesus is the Son of God he is the explicit Word of God to us, the Word that illuminates our experience. On the other hand, since he is fully human he shows a human way to respond to the mystery of God that surrounds us.

First, then, Jesus is the Word of God. Recent writers sometimes speak of him as the Sacrament, or as the Parable of God. This means that the deeds and words of Jesus, his life, death and resurrection, reveal God to us. In this individual God communicates himself to us. When we look at Jesus of Nazareth, at the way he lives and acts, at his compassion and love for sinners and outcasts, at his anger with the representations of a legalistic and institutionalized view of God, at his meals and celebrations, at the way he announces forgiveness and healing, and, above all, at the way he dies, abandoned by all on a cross, then we truly know something of God. Above all in his death and resurrection the incomprehensible and overwhelming love of God has been lavished upon us. Mercy and salvation is ours, and the promise of life that transcends death. In this particular historical person the mystery of God has been given a concrete shape. Our encounters with this Jesus challenge and sometimes shock us. They call us to radical conversion.

Jesus is the Parable of God, but as in the parables that Jesus himself tells, in him we find no neat answers about who God is. Rather he announces, in his own person, a God who is always greater than our conceptions, a God who breaks apart our tidy little worlds, a God who shows our wisdom to be foolishness. The mystery remains. Yet so much is revealed in Jesus about what kind of God God is.

If a precise grasp of the inner nature of the Father is not given to us and could not be, we do have quite clear revelation in the life of Jesus of the appropriate human response to this Father. Jesus reveals to us the way we should live our lives in fidelity to this God who is Abba and yet remains infinite mystery. His own life was a continual search for God and a continual struggle to understand God's will and to follow it in fidelity. This led finally to the total collapse of Jesus' project, to the desertion of his followers, and to the pain and loneliness of the cross.[12] And on that cross Jesus cried out: "My God, my God, why have you deserted me?" The way of Jesus certainly does not eradicate mystery. It calls for trusting surrender into the mystery. The Father's will leads to unexpected, surprising and dangerous places. The resurrection says that God's work can be accomplished even when to human eyes, including the eyes of the earthly Jesus, all that can be seen is failure.

The call to follow Jesus invites us to live out the events of each day with the same kind of creative love for our brothers and sisters that we see in Jesus, with the same sense of the mystery of God breaking in on our lives in each person and each event, with the same fidelity to the will of the Father, and with the same kind of surrender and trust in the Father's love for us.

This kind of discipleship is beyond our capabilities. It becomes possible only through the free gift of God in our lives, the Holy Spirit.

The Holy Spirit

In the Scriptures, the Spirit first appears as the breath of life, God's breath. When men and women had a religious inspiration it was attributed to a visitation from this same Spirit. The prophets were men of the Spirit. The word "breath," or "spirit," then, was used to describe God's way of touching the lives of men and women. Life itself, inspirations, prophecy, charismatic power were all attributed to the Spirit of God.

With Paul and the early Church we find the Holy Spirit everywhere. In the pre-Christian era Israel had experienced the absence of the Spirit and the rabbis awaited the gift of the Spirit in the age to come. However the early Church believed that this gift was already given through the death and resurrection of Jesus. The Church existed in the power of the Spirit.

Paul makes it clear that it is precisely because God has sent the Spirit of his Son into our heart that we can cry "Abba" (Gal 4:6). Paul's theology of the Holy Spirit is beautifully developed in Romans 5:

> Therefore, since we are justified with faith, we have peace with God through our Lord Jesus Christ. Through him we have obtained access to this grace in which we stand, and we rejoice in hope of sharing the glory of God. More than that, we rejoice in our sufferings, knowing that suffering produces endurance, and endurance produces character, and character produces hope, and hope does not disappoint us, because God's love has been poured into our hearts through the Holy Spirit who has been given to us.

"God's love has been poured into our hearts through the Holy Spirit"—this truth of salvation is central to the New Testament understanding of our personal experience of God. In this Spirit we too cry out "Abba, Father," and even our own weakness is nothing in the face of such a gift:

> Likewise the Spirit helps us in our weakness; for we do not know how to pray as we ought but the Spirit himself intercedes for us with sighs too deep for words. And he who searches the hearts of men knows what is in the mind of the Spirit, because the Spirit intercedes for the saints according to the will of God (Rom 8:26–27).

James Dunn, and others, have pointed out the direct connection in Paul between experience of the Spirit and the experience of the risen Lord Jesus.[13] From the first beginning of the Christian community the risen Lord is "source and object" of the religious experience of Christians.[14] It is the risen Lord who is experienced in the Spirit. For the Christian community it is the Lord Jesus who gives content to the experience of being in the Spirit. For the Christian experience of God is always both "dependent upon" and "derivative from" Jesus the Christ.[15]

Paul makes it abundantly clear that the religious experience of a Christian is always related to the community of believers. It is always directed toward the common life of the community. It will, if it is authentic, always build up the body of Christ in love. It always has an ecclesial dimension (1 Cor 12–14). There can be no artificial separation between experience of the risen Lord and active membership in the community that is his body.

Reflection on life reveals transcendence, mystery and a sense of the infinite at the heart of our experiences. The New Testament tells us that this mystery can be embraced with the family name "Abba," that in Jesus mystery is given a human face, and that God's love is poured out in our hearts through the Holy Spirit. Acceptance of this good news depends upon a movement of faith in the human heart. It is within the context of this faith that we continue to explore our experience of God. The presence of the indwelling Spirit is the all-important underpinning for a theological understanding of our experience of God.

five

OUR EXPERIENCE OF GOD IN THE LIGHT OF CHRISTIAN FAITH

The reflections of earlier chapters have shown that while we normally focus our attention on this or that specific person or object, yet our ordinary objective knowledge always takes place against a world of being without limit, and our love opens up toward what is beyond comprehension. Furthermore we have discussed moments in life when we may be overtaken by a sense of transcendence: experiences of love, childbirth, creativity, forgiveness, beauty, vulnerability, death, failure, loneliness and alienation. Such experiences open up to the world of transcendence, but of themselves they remain obscure and leave us with many questions. What is the connection between such experiences and the explicit revelation given in Jesus Christ?

Before attempting to answer this question in detail it might be helpful to consider the difference between implicit and explicit awareness and love in an ordinary relationship. Anthony and Sue are two individuals teaching on a large school staff. They have worked together for some years and share many interests, including a real commitment to their students. There are many projects on which they have collaborated happily together. They have learned to trust and respect each other. Each thinks of the other as a friend. One night, after they have spent some time together at a party, Sue goes home with a vague sense of unease and with some confused feelings about her relationship with Anthony. After a few days she decides to talk with him about how she feels. She tells him that he is becoming more and more important to her. Anthony is surprised by this revelation and takes a while to absorb it. He begins to recognize that similar feelings have been building up in him, although he has paid them little attention. Sue and Anthony decide that they matter immensely to each other. They come to declare their love for each other. After this life changes for both of them. What was a vague, general feeling of friendship and trust becomes a passionate commitment. The relationship grows and deepens over months and years of life. They look back on that first declaration of love as the major turning point in their lives. Yet in retrospect they know that even before this declaration there was real love between them, more than they had explicitly recognized. The explicit expression of love changes everything, yet it expresses what was, in some way, already present.

While there are some major differences between God's self-communication to us and the relationship between Anthony and Sue, yet it seems to me that the analogy is helpful, at least in a general way; it offers a way of understanding the connection and the difference between our experience of God in the moments of transcendence in our lives, and the explicit revelation we are given in the Gospel of Jesus. It is the difference between an implicit knowledge and love of another and an explicit relationship. Perhaps it will be helpful, at this point, to examine what the New Testament tells us about our implicit experiences of transcendence, and to follow this by a discussion of the relationship between such implicit awareness and explicit faith in Jesus Christ.

Experiences of "Mystery" and "Grace" in the Light of the New Testament

If we ask what the New Testament tells us about the experience of mystery that is so central to our lives, then we must look to that word by which Jesus addresses God, "Abba." Here we find something that is not at all evident from a reflection on human experience: the mystery is a mystery of incomprehensible love. Our sense of mystery opens out in the direction of the one who can be named Abba. Furthermore, this Abba is radically involved with us as persons, and calls us into love and service of each other. The mystery that surrounds us points to unconditional love, to which we can surrender ourselves in total trust.

What the Gospel proclaims, then, is that the whole of life is upheld and encompassed by a God who loves us passionately. This God surrounds us at every turn in a horizon of love. The whole of reality is personal. The universe is friendly. This claim of the New Testament does not deny the reality and the horror of war, starvation, oppression and death. It does not deny the evil that is in the hearts of men and women. It puts before us the cross of Jesus in all its starkness, but it makes the astounding claim that death does not have the last word. In the face of both the pain and the joy of our lives the New Testament challenges us with its good news. It claims that the source and goal of the mystery in our lives is not cold and distant but is warm and gracious, and turns to us with a love that knows no conditions or reservations. The only barrier to this love is sin, our own choice to reject it.

Jesus reveals that we, like him, can reach out into mystery and cry out "Abba." It is in him, his life, death and resurrection, that we see the face of God. In and through him, we are taken into the life of the Trinity. Like him we too are called to be open to the ways in which God touches our lives through the Holy Spirit. In the light of the New Testament we can affirm that the risen Lord himself is present to us through this Spirit poured out in our lives.

It is precisely here that we find the connection between the New Testament and the experiences of grace that have already been discussed. They were initially called moments of "grace" because they are times when we experience something given, from beyond ourselves, as a free gift. In the light of the New Testament we know these gifts to be the work in us of the Holy Spirit. These can be called experiences of grace, not now simply because they come upon us as a gift, but because they are the gift of God himself, present and active in our lives. Grace is God communicating himself to us in the Spirit, freely loving us, forgiving us, inviting us into relationship with him and calling us to the transformation of the world as disciples of Jesus.[1]

In this gift we find peace and reconciliation. It is in this gift of the Holy Spirit that we too cry out "Abba." It is in this Spirit of Jesus Christ that we find our salvation. This offer of love is always present to us, needing only our own free choice to accept what is freely given. This transforming grace can be thwarted only by our free choice to exclude it from our lives.

Does everyone receive this gift of God present in grace? Does everyone experience, in some way, this Holy Spirit present in his or her life? The answer to both these questions must be a clear "yes." It is true that over the years there has been a tendency to describe God's grace as restricted to those who belong to the Christian Church.[2] However, this teaching has never done justice to God's will to save all men and women, a truth clearly taught in the New Testament.[3] One of the most important theological developments enshrined in the documents of the Second Vatican Council is the unambiguous claim that God's grace is available to all men and women and this saving love cannot be kept within any boundaries.[4]

All of this is saying that all men and women, as they live out their own existence, know and love in a world of grace. This God, present in grace, is the backdrop and the horizon for our everyday life. Rahner uses two beautiful images to speak of this. That to which we give our attention in our lives is like a tiny island surrounded by a boundless ocean of nameless Mystery.[5] Again, just as we see things by the light of the sun, without exactly seeing the light or attending to it, so we know and love in our everyday lives in the light of the experience of grace, which may not be explicitly noticed or conceptualized.[6]

In the light of Christian revelation, then, our experiences of mystery and of moments of grace in our lives can properly be seen for what they are, the experience of a God who is Father, Son and Holy Spirit. It is Jesus himself who enables us to come to know the Father as the hidden goal of the mystery of our lives. It is in his Spirit that we cry out "Abba." It is the Spirit of Jesus who breaks in upon our lives at those moments when we are surprised by the sense of gift, and our eyes are opened in awe and wonder.

The experience of mystery that is always present in our lives, if often not noticed, is truly called an experience of God in the sense that it opens out toward the one whom we have been taught to call Abba. It is not that the experience of being without limits can be equated with God's inner being. We do not experience the inner being of God. However, the mystery that we do experience is penetrated and transformed by the presence of God in grace, and the experience of mystery opens us up in unknowing, to the Father of Jesus.

The experiences of grace in special moments of life are truly called experiences of God in that they are movements in us of the Holy Spirit, the Spirit of Jesus. They are ways in which God speaks to us through persons and events. Those times of, for example, simple joy in the humanity of another person, which leave us with a sense of wonder and thankfulness, are truly blessed times in that in them we are open to the Spirit of God in a unique way. We can dwell in these moments and then they can become true prayer, but this needs to be dealt with more explicitly in a later section of this book.

Experience of God and Explicit Faith

Reflection on the New Testament and what it can tell us about experience of God raises a further question: If we can and do experience God in the grace that is poured out in our lives, how does this experience connect with the objective historical revelation of God in the life, death and resurrection of Jesus, with the New Testament proclamation, and the Church's preaching and practice?

St. Augustine's way of dealing with this question is to speak to two missions of the Blessed Trinity. One is the exterior mission by which the Son and the Spirit were sent at a specific point in history (in the incarnation and the first Pentecost); the other is the interior mission to the individual soul. Augustine clearly believes that we experience the Trinitarian visitations in our own hearts. He cannot conceive of a mission which a person is unable to perceive.[7] Thomas Aquinas, commenting on Augustine, speaks of a kind of experiential knowledge of the indwelling Trinity. This awareness of God's presence is, according to Thomas, a gift of the Holy Spirit, the gift of wisdom. It is an awareness we have through our union in love with God, a knowledge through love.[8]

Augustine and Aquinas agree that God communicates himself both interiorly, through the action of the Holy Spirit, and exteriorly in Jesus Christ and the events of salvation history.[9] The two are, of course, intimately connected. When we experience God present in our lives through the gift of grace, it is clear that this grace is given to us in and through Jesus Christ. Both the internal experience of grace and the exterior revelation in Jesus are necessary. Theology and catechesis cannot afford to emphasize one without the other. When this happens, and it often has in our history, Christian life suffers.

Personal experience of mystery, without the explicit good news of Jesus Christ, is not enough. Of itself the experience remains obscure and mysterious. The experience of transcendence can be interpreted in many ways; this is clear from the various religious positions that men and women actually take up. A man may experience transcendence in his life, live out his life according to his conscience, and yet still remain agnostic. There is no doubt that such a man can be saved by God's grace. Yet the man's life, though lived with integrity, is drastically impoverished.

He is like a lonely man who hungers for another person to share his life, and who lives his whole life with a general and unspoken attraction for a woman of his acquaintance. She, however, loves him with passion and tenderness, and unable to hold back her love, she declares it explicitly in a message which manifests what is in her heart. Yet the man never recognizes the message for what it is and continues to live his good, but empty life, with only a general sense of mutual awareness and attraction between himself and the woman.

Experience of mystery and transcendence needs the illumination of the Gospel in order that a person can know the gift that is being given and be challenged to respond with a whole new relationship with God and a whole new way of life. The preaching of the Church and its doctrine is needed because experience of mystery and moments of grace cannot, of themselves, offer us the good news of what kind of God God is. This is revealed only in Jesus and it is embraced in explicit faith in him, within a community of believing disciples.[10]

On the other hand, the explicit preaching or teaching of the Gospel (or Church doctrine) is of no use unless it touches the place where God is already communicating himself in a person's heart.[11] As Thomas Aquinas pointed out long ago, the growth of faith in a person needs not only the exterior prompting of the preacher but the more important interior action of the Holy Spirit.[12]

The attempt to evangelize only through transfer of explicit doctrine from one person to another is doomed to failure. A Christian woman who would share her faith with a friend would best begin by listening to her friend at depth. To take seriously the experience of the friend, to listen attentively and receive it as a gift, is already to share one's faith. The listener is communicating her sense of reverence for what is occurring in her friend's experience, already saying implicitly: "This is the place of grace." If the woman can enable her friend to notice mystery and grace in her life, then the explicit Gospel message can bring illumination, joy, and the possibility of real conversion.

The process of preaching the Gospel must always respect the twofold nature of God's self-communication. The One who is revealed to us explicitly in Jesus is already communicating himself obscurely to those who are yet to hear the Gospel for the first time. The preacher of the Gospel must know that what is being preached is already known in an obscure way by those who are listening, since their lives are lived in a world of grace.

Some Characteristics of Our Experience of God

Perhaps we are in a position now to gather together some elements that might point to what in our lives can be called correctly an experience of God. What makes an experience truly an experience of God, rather than simply, for example, an experience of beauty? At a later time it will be important to return to this question and attempt to make a list of defining characteristics of the experience of God. It is important at this stage to gather together some considerations that emerge from the discussion to this point.

In the first place it can be said that any genuine experience of God will resonate with what we learn from the Gospels.[13] For a Christian all experience of God depends upon and is in some way derivative from Jesus' own experience of his Father as Abba. Jesus' own encounter with his Father drew him into a life of intimate union with his Father which meant hours and nights of prayer and a lifelong hunger to do his Father's will. It impelled him to preach the reign of God, announce forgiveness, bring healing, condemn and struggle against evil, and stand with the outcasts of his society. It led him to accept his death and gave him hope that the Father would bring life out of failure. If Jesus himself is God's Word to us, then our experience of God will be an experience that his life, death and resurrection can illuminate and transform. Our experience of God will be an experience of the risen Lord, an experience given in his Spirit.

This means several things. The community of the Church is the sacrament of Jesus' presence in the world. It is to be presumed, then, that experience of God will not cut one off from the community of believers, but rather lead a person in the direction of fidelity to the community and the tradition. It is possible, of course, and to be expected, that genuine experience of God may lead to a prophetic stance against abuses in the Church. However this does not deny, but rather affirm, that such experience opens us toward an uncompromising love of the Church.

If our experience of God is tested against Jesus and his Gospel it will mean, as well, that two poles, relationship with God and with men and women in the world, will be held together. It will open us toward a deeper union with God. It will lead us in the direction of a more total commitment of ourselves to our brothers and sisters. In Johannes Metz's terms it will be both "mystical and political" in its orientation.[14] These two terms suggest two aspects of experience of God that will need to be more fully developed in following chapters.

Another characteristic of human experience of God is that it is always an experience of gift.[15] Whatever the human situation in which this mysterious event occurs, it becomes (as the name suggests) an experience of grace when we know that we are receiving a gift, and that this moment of life is not explainable by chance or by one's own efforts, but must be received humbly as given to us. Two people might watch a sunrise. For both it may be an experience of overwhelming beauty. It might be an experience of God for one person and not for the other, because the first person receives it as a gift while the second has no sense of its being a personal gift.

This sense of gift is very close to two other characteristics of the experience of God. The first of these is the sense of transcendence. The experience is always one of something beyond our powers and beyond our comprehension. It breaks in upon our normal world and opens us out into a world that is beyond us. It is always an experience of "going beyond" our normal categories.

This leads to another characteristic, the sense of mystery. This is linked directly with the experience that a particular event is a gift and a moment of transcendence. It is always an obscure experience and a subtle one, an experience that our intellects are unable to dominate. This mysterious, elusive character or our experience of God is well caught in the story from 1 Kings where Elijah finds the Lord not in the great strong wind that breaks up mountains, nor in the violence of earthquake or fire, but in the whispering of gentle breezes.[16] John of the Cross tells us that the experience of grace is subtle and mysterious, "like the whispering of love-stirring breezes."[17] We are unable to pin it down or to say too much about it. We cannot even express it to ourselves without making it concrete, and this means that much of what we have experienced has escaped our conceptualization.

While the experience of God is always one of transcendence and mystery, it is also true that it always occurs in and through ordinary human experience. God is found at the heart of what is human. It is always an experience of immanence. The discussion in earlier chapters of the experience of mystery and the instances given of experience of grace reveal that God is encountered precisely in our human existence in the world.

Finally, there is the question whether immediacy is a characteristic of our experience of God. Can this experience be best described as mediate or immediate? This question has been much debated through the years, and contemporary theologians can seem to do no better than to speak of a "mediated immediacy."[18] While this language is not very satisfying, it indicates that we are dealing with an experience which transcends our normal categories. In the light of the reflections we have so far made concerning our experiences of God, it seems to me that we must come to the conclusion that the experience can be called immediate from one point of view and mediated from several other points of view.

The experience is immediate in that it occurs without any sense of an intermediary between the individual and the God who is present by grace. There is a sense of God's closeness which occurs without the mediations of concept, image or word. It is a sense of presence and of union which occurs at a pre-conceptual level. Thomas Aquinas teaches that while our intellects in this life cannot know God as he is in himself, yet we can love him in himself.[19] By charity the soul is united immediately to God.[20] There can, then, be a loving union with God that has a certain immediacy, and the experience of grace is precisely such an experience of loving union occurring at a pre-conceptual level.

However from other points of view, the experience of grace must be seen as mediated. First it is always mediated because it occurs in and through everyday experience. We experience grace in and through the events of our lives. It arises in and through, for example, our love for another person, or the death of a friend, and it is in a real sense mediated by these occurrences.

There is also the further mediation that occurs in the process of becoming aware of the encounter. My own experience of grace becomes available to me through the mediations of my own consciousness. The experiential encounter is inevitably interpreted in consciousness through the mediations of concept, image and word. Without this mediation there is no possibility of any awareness of an encounter.

What might be said then is that although grace is experienced through the mediation of everyday occurrences in our life, yet when this God of grace is experienced as present to us, then there is a sense of union with God without intermediaries. We can have an immediate sense of God's presence, but this occurs in and through the mediation of an ordinary human event and depends upon the further mediation of our own interpreting consciousness.

six

THE SOCIAL STRUCTURE
OF EXPERIENCE OF GOD

The theological approach to experience of God which has been argued in these pages needs, at this point, to be developed in two directions: on the one hand, it must be shown how such experience of God relates to society and history (the social structure, treated in this chapter); on the other hand, it must be shown how experience of God opens out into contemplative prayer (the mystical dimension, treated in the next chapter).

There is an urgent need, in this last part of the twentieth century, to attend to the social and historical structure of our experience of God. We have become aware how easily our theology and our Church practice can become "privatized."[1] Such a privatized Christianity can be seen in its extreme form where military leaders who are responsible for repression, torture and death on a massive scale attend Eucharist on Sundays with a tranquil conscience. It is seen closer to home where active Church members see no contradiction between their faith and their support for policies which take for granted widespread unemployment, the possibility of irreversible damage to our environment, and the exaltation of the arms race. These Christians usually maintain that religion should be kept out of the public arena. It should not seek to influence "professional" areas of life like economic policy. It is strictly a private matter.

Where faith becomes privatized it is properly subject to the critique of Marx. He argues that religion, through its emphasis on the world of transcendence, lifts the eyes of the poor from the real misery of their historical existence and enables them to accept their lot in life. Religious faith then exercises a conservative social function; it helps to maintain the social order as it is, with all its structural injustice.[2]

There can be no quarrel with this critique when it is applied not to faith in general, but to a privatized Christianity. It cannot be denied that there has been a tendency, in some twentieth century theology, to focus on an individualistic stance before God. This kind of theology has reinforced a middle-class religion, which has offered no serious resistance to social injustice, and which has functioned in such a way as to legitimize the present economic system.

Some theologians, in reaction to this "privatized" theology, have a tendency to retreat from a reflection on transcendence in life, in order to stress exclusively the concrete, the social and the historical dimensions of Christian life in the world.[3] There can be no quarrel with the attention given to these last three dimensions of life. Such a concentration is essential. However to abandon the theological task of articulating the mystery of transcendence at the heart of the concrete, social and historical dimensions of human life is to throw the baby out with the bath water.

The argument should not be around the question whether theology should best attend to history or to transcendence. This is an entirely false dilemma. The central task of theology is to reflect upon and to articulate (in the light of the Gospel) the transcendent dimensions of human history. The problem in a "privatized theology" is not its concern with transcendence, but that this transcendence is understood as occurring in a subject who is seen exclusively as an individual.[4] The correction of this tendency is in the development of a theology which can show how moments of mystery and ultimacy occur in their proper fullness when the individual is seen as he or she is in truth, as a person in society, shaped and formed by a history of relationships, at the mercy of enormous social forces, and able to make some response to all of this.[5] As well as this, theology must show how the God of Jesus Christ is a God who breaks in upon our lives in a way which calls for transformation of our world. Such a God cannot be domesticated.

It is important, then, to spell out in more detail how the kind of reflection that has already been done in earlier sections of this work relates to history and the social order. This will mean showing more explicitly how the experience of God always occurs within history and within the network of social relationships. It will mean showing that the experience of God, where it is accurately interpreted, will always have social effects that are humanizing and liberating. Then it will be appropriate to turn to one key experience which most radically moves us beyond a "privatized" theology—the experience of God in the poor.

The Historical Nature of Experience of God

It has been said many times that the experience of mystery occurs as the horizon for our encounter with other beings in the world. It arises, above all, in our experience of other men and women in our world. This experience occurs as we live out the events of our personal existence. It occurs in and through history.

The experience of God is always directly related to our engagement in the world. However the connection between God and history is not simply that God is experienced in and through our personal history. Rather it must be insisted that the experience of God transforms our sense of history and time. Far from leading us away from our history, the experience of God can give a whole new meaning to our time. It can lead from the experience of time as *chronos* to the experience of time as *kairos*.

— *Chronos* usually refers to the mere sequence of seconds, minutes and hours that can be empirically measured, while *kairos* refers to time that is full of human meaning. Jesus began his preaching with the words: "The time (*kairos*) has come." *Kairos* is the time of salvation, of the in-breaking of God's kingdom, of the experience of grace.[6]

The experience of God arises in specific events in our lives, and then changes our perception of these events so that they can be perceived as full of meaning. The experience of God may occur, for example, in a relationship with another person. Far from being a distraction from the knowing and loving of the other person, the experience of God actually gives full human significance to the relationship. It enables the other person to be received as a gift. Its function is to deepen the relationship and place it in an ultimate context. The experience of God might also occur in a strike, in the solidarity that occurs when men and women struggle together to change unjust working conditions. When this solidarity is experienced as grace, it does not remove a person from the arena of the struggle for justice. Rather it reveals the full meaning of the event and enables deeper commitment and provides a source of courage and energy.

Needless to say, this experience of God does not simply confirm what is already occurring in our lives. It may reveal a call in what we are already doing which invites us to go far beyond our present level of commitment. It may also disrupt our present position and call it into question and challenge us to redirection. Grace calls us into the future—God's future.

The experience of God, then, allows us to become more fully alive, more fully human and more thoroughly and passionately involved in our human history. But what of society and politics? How does the experience of God relate to these realities?

The Social Structure of the Experience of God

First of all it is important to recall again that the experience of grace occurs precisely in social experience. The reflection that we have made on our knowing and loving has shown that we experience mystery precisely when we move beyond ourselves toward other human beings.

However another question must be asked: Cannot this experience of God still be entirely individualistic? Can it not be simply something that arises in a meeting of two people alone, with no connections with the social order? This can be answered (1) by reflection on the social nature of our personal encounters, (2) by examining the experience of God that occurs in groups, and (3) by reflecting on the One that we encounter in an experience of grace.

To think that we exist and relate to each other as isolated individuals is to misunderstand completely the nature of human existence. We are not self-sufficient and complete individuals who may decide at a certain time to enter into relationships with other individuals. We only become who we are through the networks of relationships that shape our lives. We are first in relationship and then we know ourselves as a center of consciousness apart from those to whom we relate. Every time we move into a new encounter with another person we come as people shaped by a history of relationships. We inhabit a culture, a world-view, a complex pattern of thoughts and tastes that has been shaped by our relationships.

Both consciously and unconsciously we have absorbed a framework for our lives. This framework is, to a large extent, socially determined, but it becomes internalized within us.[7] Such a framework will contain a whole host of assumptions. Some of these assumptions might be: it is important to make as much money as possible; assessment of people is to be made in terms of the kind of house and car they own; it is important to be competitive and to emerge from the contests of life as victor; it is natural and proper for some to be extremely wealthy while others starve; totalitarian repression can be justified for the "good of the people"; the economic system of international capitalism can be justified because it is necessary to preserve freedom and democracy; war is justifiable when the leaders of the country decide it is necessary or it is in defense of some principle. It would be easy to draw up a list of contrary assumptions that might be socially communicated, assumptions closer to the Gospel of Jesus Christ. However the point at issue is our experience of God. This arises in our relationships with other persons, but these relationships are never between isolated individuals who are influenced by nothing beyond themselves. Our world is a world of social and political forces which have influenced our own persons to such an extent that we internalize the values of the social order. So a black man in a white-dominated country may have to struggle with his own internalization of the assumption of white superiority. So women around the world are struggling against their own internalizing of the assumption of male superiority in certain key areas of life.

The experience of grace occurs in the heart of a person who lives completely immersed in the network of social relationships and in the world of politics.[8] The problem is that these social connections and influences may not be visible to the individual. In fact it is often to the advantage of those in control of the world of economics and politics that these socially communicated assumptions are kept well hidden.

First, then, the experience of grace has a social structure because individuals bring to the encounter a self shaped by relationships and social forces. Second, it is important to notice that we often experience God precisely in our experience of groups. When we gather in a small community to reflect about our lives, to listen to the Gospel of Jesus, to support each other in action, to pray together, we might well feel that here we experience

God's grace. This experience of the dawning kingdom of God certainly has social effects that are liberating. It gives us insight into what true community, and a society based on respect, cooperation and love, might look like. It calls into question the pattern of our economic and social orders which maintain injustice and exploitation. Such a social experience of grace enables us to see more starkly the reality of social sin, which dominates so many of our cultural and social patterns, and it also gives us the hope we need to confront these sinful social structures and to take action against them. Such liberating experiences of God occur not only in our assembly as Christians, but in all kinds of experiences of social groups which open out into the world of mystery and grace. Grace is present at the heart of our experience of community and solidarity. This theme will be mentioned again in the discussion of the ways in which we experience God in the poor. Here it is important to stress two things: the experience of grace illuminates the signs of the kingdom of God already present in our social communion and calls us in this direction; it also manifests the darkness and sin of our social order and calls us to social transformation.[9]

The third, and most important, argument for the social structure of the experience of grace comes from a reflection on the One who is encountered. Whether the experience of grace occurs in a very personal encounter or in an experience of community, it always has a social structure because of the God who is experienced.

If there had been no revelation in Jesus Christ and if there had been no Gospel, then, perhaps, we could experience transcendence and mystery without these having a major social impact. Even this statement becomes debatable when we look at the way in which various religions connect transcendence with social ethics. However when a person experiences grace as a follower of Jesus, then what is experienced is not some nameless mystery, but the One to whom Jesus cried out "Abba." What

Christians experience is given content by the revelation in Jesus Christ; for the disciple the experience of grace receives its authentic interpretation in the light of the Gospel.

This Holy One who is experienced is the God of Jesus, the One whose liberating reign Jesus announced in word and deed. This is the One who is radically involved with human beings, a God whose passion is our salvation. This is the God of sinners and outcasts, the God of the Poor, the God who reveals himself to us in the cross of Jesus.

To meet this God in truth is to have one's socially ordered universe shattered and transformed. Such a God calls our social institutions and our socially-induced assumptions into question. It is not easy to hold onto an assumption that one's race, class or sex is superior, or to an ethic of competition and success, or to possessive materialism when the One we encounter is the Crucified. The experience of grace is a dangerous encounter in which our world can be turned on its head. Everything now is tested against love since the One encountered is love. Experience of this God is subversive.

Experience of God, whether it occurs in an encounter between individuals or in an experience of a group, always has a social structure and can always have a liberating effect on our lives. It can show up the subtle processes by which we have internalized values contrary to the kingdom of God and call these into question. This grace reveals the infinite value of human persons. It shows us both the gifts and the evil that is institutionalized in our social structures.

All our experiences which open out into the mystery of grace should impel us in the direction of full human liberation. That this often fails to occur can be explained only by the fact that we are closed to the truth that is so close to us—we have not eyes to see or ears to hear. We are in need of a jolt to our complacency that can call us to a new conversion. Such a jolt occurs in our experience of the poor of our world. This experience of the poor must be considered a privileged path to liberating experience of God.

Experience of God in the Poor

In Israel in the time of Jesus there were many pious people who belonged to prestigious religious groups (the priests and the Sadducees, the scribes and the Pharisees, the Essenes, even the Zealots). These groups had one thing in common: they set themselves completely apart from sinners. In fact they tended to look on all those outside their groups as sinners. It seems to be a pattern in human life that when people belong to a demanding organization they experience a need to look down on those who are excluded. This is true of religious groups as much as any other, and it was true in a particular way of the various religious establishments within early first century Judaism.[10]

These groups of religious men excluded the public sinners (such as the tax collectors, the prostitutes, and those who practiced dishonest trades), those who suffered misfortune (the lepers, the possessed, the blind, the lame), those whose ancestry was "illegitimate," the poor, and the ignorant who did not even know the law, let alone keep it.[11] By and large they also excluded women, or, at least, kept them in an inferior position.

Any kind of analysis of the society in which Jesus lived would show this gap between the religious (and social) insiders and those who were despised as outcasts. Jesus totally rejected these values of his contemporaries. While he did not exclude from his company the rich or those who belonged to prestigious groups (he certainly showed his care for them as individuals), yet he did make a particular choice in his life to ally himself with sinners and outsiders. His vocation was to be with the "lost sheep of the house of Israel" (see Mt 9:36; 10:6; 15:24, Lk 15).

Jesus made it clear that he stood with those lost ones by his healing, by his declaration of forgiveness, by seeking their company and above all by sharing meals with them. His preaching declared that the poor were blessed and that the lost ones were God's chief concern.

This choice of Jesus must be traced back to his own encounter with God. The God of Jesus, who could be named "Abba," was a God on the side of humanity in general and on the side of the outcasts and the lost ones in particular.[12] This is the kind of God that is imaged in the parables of the lost sheep, the lost coin and the lost son. Jesus went to the lost ones because it was to them that he had been "sent"—this mission was determined by his own encounter with his Father.

All of this is suggesting that for Jesus and for his followers experience of God is intimately linked to experience of the poor. Experience of the God of Jesus impels us toward the poor. However it is also true that the poor are a privileged place of access to the God of Jesus. The poor are blessed. The writer of Matthew's Gospel summarizes this: in our encounter with the hungry, the thirsty, the strangers, the naked, the sick and the prisoners of our world we are encountering the Lord (Mt 25:31–46).

The experience of God in the poor can sometimes be a troubling and painful experience, and at other times it can be a time of deep joy and peace. In this it reflects the pattern of experience of God in general. In the writings of John of the Cross we find that while union with God is sometimes imaged as the dark night of suffering,[13] at other times it is imaged as the beautiful and peaceful time before the sun rises—"the tranquil night at the time of the rising dawn."[14] John of the Cross asks himself why the inflow of God is sometimes experienced as painful and other times as joy and delight. He finds that the reason is not in God himself. God always approaches us with love. If we experience pain in this presence instead of peace and joy, it can only be caused by incongruity between ourselves and our God. Our hearts are not attuned to such a gift but are more at home with what is not of God. The pain is the pain of disharmony, the pain that comes from lack of congruence. When our hearts become attuned to this gift and our lives are in congruence with this God, then the experience is one of integration and joy.[15] Experience of God in the poor, too, can sometimes be an experience of harmony and congruence, while at other times the experience is of painful incongruence.

Experience of God in the poor is sometimes a painful dark night to us and sometimes it is the beautiful illumination and warmth of the dawn. Experiences of dark night (where there is lack of congruence) include (1) the experience of a guilty conscience, (2) our helplessness before the power of oppression, and (3) loneliness and failure. These experiences, I want to argue, must be seen as genuine encounters with God, even though they are so dark and negative. Like the classic "dark night" of John of the Cross it is in them that we can experience the "inflow of God." Experiences of the beautiful night as dawn breaks (where there is congruity) include (1) the experience of a gift given to us in the poor, (2) the experience of solidarity with others in the struggle for justice, and (3) the experience of action. Both kinds of experience, I want to suggest, are equally experiences of God. It might be helpful to consider these six experiences in more detail.

The Guilty Conscience

Many Christians today find themselves with a guilty conscience about the poor. There are many reasons for this. We are confronted each day with the sufferings of others in our world through newspapers, radio and television. We live in a culture which has begun to understand the mechanisms of exploitation. Many of us now have some awareness that we belong to an affluent minority of the people of the world and that our consumption and wealth is directly related to the poverty of others.

A new emphasis in Christology has also contributed to this "guilty conscience." We have begun again to look at Jesus of Nazareth and the particular options he made in his life. Jesus' own love for the poor, his choice to be with the "lost ones" and his death among the outcasts have become a powerful challenge to many in the Christian community.

Because of these factors and others some Christians find themselves today in real anguish. They know in themselves an undeniable sense of call to imitate Jesus by a concrete identification with those who suffer most in our society. But this, perhaps, goes along with a feeling of being trapped in an affluent life style. There may be real responsibilities that appear to bind these persons where they are. Because of commitments already undertaken it may not be at all clear what can be done. And yet there is a strong restless urge that is saying that something must be done. Such persons may feel very uneasy with their own affluence and the whole pattern of their lives.

There is a real disharmony and alienation between the life that is being led and the deepest yearning of the heart. There is a lack of integration between the concrete life of the person and his or her sense of the direction of God's call.

It must be insisted that this pain is a real experience of God. It is tempting to put it aside and obscure it in busyness and the distractions that our society so readily provides. However we are invited to enter this particularly contemporary dark night and in this experience of our own weakness find something of the mystery of God. This unsettling awareness of the plight of our brothers and sisters and of our own poor response is truly of God, and it is one of the clearly authentic ways in which we hear his Word in our time.

This kind of "guilty conscience" is a great blessing, and it is important to recognize it as such. It is an invitation to set out, like Abraham of old, on a pilgrimage of faith even though there may be no clear sense of the final destination. Even the first steps may not be evident, and there may be a call to continue searching or a need simply to wait until the direction becomes clear, without closing one's heart to this insistent demand.

To allow ourselves to hear the cry of the poor in this unsettling way is to experience God in our lives.

Encounter with the Poor

Often the step beyond the experience of "guilty conscience" is the simple act of encountering those whom our society excludes. It occurs, perhaps, in meeting a woman who has been left alone to bring up her children, with a constant battle for survival on her hands in an environment in which drugs, crime and hopelessness are part of life; perhaps it happens in time spent with a child who lives with a physical or psychological handicap. Such moments can be truly times of grace in our lives, times when we are given the mysterious gift of knowing the Holy One in this person before us.

In the encounter with the poor we learn something about life, about what it is to be a man or woman, about the mystery that surrounds our life and about our stance before our God. There is something, a Word of God, that can be heard only from the "little ones" of the earth. The living contact with the poor brings us to a sense of our own poverty and of our common humanity.

Jean Vanier's way of expressing this is to say that the poor are always prophetic. They have a word of God for us, a word that we need. But we need to take time to listen and to learn: "That means staying near them, because they speak quietly and infrequently; they are afraid to speak because they have been broken and oppressed."[16]

In Latin America this truth has been expressed by saying that the poverty of the people is the new spiritual master of the disciple of Jesus. It is the poor who lead the disciple toward a new encounter with God. Just as the great writers of spirituality of the past can lead us to God, and as the spiritual directors of today lead us to authentic prayer, so the poor can be our spiritual directors opening us up in a new and essential way to the mystery of God.[17]

Where we are blessed with such an experience, then our alienation is overcome and we know our God and ourselves in a moment of authenticity and truth.

Helplessness Before the Forces of Oppression

A person may move beyond the call of God in the experience of a "guilty conscience" to a real involvement with the poor only to find that this leads to the pain of helplessness. This is the result of the awareness of the sheer size of the problem of poverty, the knowledge of some of its causes and the feeling that nothing can be done.

Confronted with the powerful mechanisms that control society, with the insidious myths by which the social order is legitimized, and with the seeming impossibility of change, the temptation is to bitterness and hopelessness. This is the time when it is easy to withdraw and to give one's energy to some less demanding concern.

However this must be unmasked as a temptation to abandon the real cross of Christian existence in the world. The seductive voices of "common sense" suggest that there is no point in standing out against the tide. These voices have great power because they are the voices of respectability in our kind of social order. To stand with the poorest in our society means standing against the weight of the forces that control society. These forces have tentacles that reach deep into those we love, and into our own beings. Because of this there may be an experience of disharmony and alienation with those who are closest to us. We may experience this alienation as a split within ourselves.

Its root cause may be seen as the lack of congruity between a stance with the poor and the pull of the society which shapes us.

If, however, we can stay with our helplessness before the power of evil, and still attempt to live each day creatively and lovingly, then God can be found in the darkness. In our very poverty and inability to do much we learn that everything does not depend on us. We begin to discern in this experience the mysterious ground of our hope. To enter this dark night, and not run from it, is to experience God in our lives.

Action

Perhaps we underestimate action as a place where God is experienced in our lives. Certainly in our tradition, contemplation has often been opposed to the active life. Of course there have also been serious attempts at describing (and living) a spirituality which is "contemplative in action." The concept of contemplation in action is an extremely important one, referring to a contemplative stance before the whole of our active lives. This is indispensable for a contemporary spirituality. However I would like to go beyond this concept to discuss those moments when actually doing something in the case of justice is transparently a moment of grace.

Our philosophers and theologians often write as if the human person is sufficiently described in terms of intellect and will. Africans have described Europeans as people who use their bodies to carry their heads around. We tend to underestimate the moments when we do and act, when we labor to create and transform. Christian spirituality needs to recover the awareness that we can meet our God not only in and through our knowledge and our love of others, but in a special way in our acting and doing. In fact love reaches its full human potential only when it does express itself in action.

When we act in the cause of justice there are times when

such action is in line with our deepest sense of ourselves. The action itself is in harmony with the dimension of our existence where our beings are touched by the mystery of God. This action itself is a real moment of grace.

In taking concrete action for justice we find ourselves as human beings and there is real joy in the integrity of inner conviction and lived reality. The result of this congruence, between our actions and the stirrings of the Spirit within, is that we actually experience the fruits of the Holy Spirit—peace, love and joy. These fruits are not added gifts. They are simply what result when our acting selves are transparent to the Holy Spirit. They occur when we find ourselves acting in tune with the movements of God in the depths of our beings.[18] The joy of this kind of authenticity leads us to thanksgiving, in the knowledge that it is a most precious gift.

Loneliness and Failure

There are times when our plans come to nothing and our actions fail. There are times when we know that we have failed as individuals and we find ourselves overwhelmed by our own selfishness or cowardice.

One of the most difficult experiences occurs when the very people to whom we would hope to reach out reject the offer that is made. Perhaps the poor see through the pretensions of our Christian charity. Perhaps they associate Christians with the groups that exploit and oppress them. They too can manipulate and hit back.

There is no joy in such encounters. Then we are thrown back on our own aloneness and find ourselves, perhaps, without resources. Karl Rahner speaks powerfully to this experience of radical loneliness.

When we go to meet this wretched neighbor in the way that we should, when we care about him without any supporting feeling of instinctive, physiologically conditioned sympathy, when we forgive even while feeling that we are being made fools of by doing so, when we really pour ourselves out without the reward of a feeling of satisfaction and without any return in gratitude, when our very encounter with our neighbor makes us unutterably lonely and all such love seems to be only an annihilating leap into an absolute void, then that is really God's hour in our life; that is when he is there. Assuming that we don't turn back, assuming that it doesn't get us down, that we don't find ourselves some sort of compensation elsewhere, that we don't complain, that we don't feel sorry for ourselves, that we keep quiet about it and really accept and commit ourselves to the absence of ground under our feet and the foolishness of such love, then it is God's hour; then this seemingly sinister abyss in our existence, as it opens up in this hopeless experience of our neighbor, will be the abyss of God himself, communicating himself to us; it will be the beginning of the coming of his infinity, where all roads disappear, and which feels like nothingness because it is infinity.[19]

Rahner comments that this experience may seem alien to us, and we may need to flee back to safer territory but gradually we can learn to find "life in this death, intimacy in this loneliness, God in this forsakenness."[20]

Solidarity

The sense of powerlessness that can occur in action for justice has already been discussed. Standing alongside the poorest will usually place the Christian in a "cognitive minority." As has been said, this in itself can open us into the mystery of God.

However it also calls us together in love. We are able to support each other in the struggle through acting together, reflecting together, sharing joys and tensions, relaxing together, sharing meals and celebrations and praying for and with each other.

Where Christians gather, as followers of Jesus, to engage in reflection on their lives and to take action on behalf of their brothers and sisters, there is something boundless and unmistakably of God in the communion of discipleship. Jesus' promise becomes a matter of actual experience: "Where two or three are gathered in my name, there am I in the midst of them." We can gather in his name in many ways, but there is a special sense of his presence when we gather in the name and in the cause of the poorest in our community. The solidarity of those engaged in the struggle for justice is a privileged place for our experience of God's grace. Where this solidarity in the search for justice is also a communion of those who surrender their lives to God in Christian prayer, then such a meeting of persons is a true experience of the Holy Spirit.

In this kind of solidarity and community there is a depth that opens out into the love of our God. It is this love which is the common ground between us.

seven

MYSTICAL EXPERIENCE OF GOD

It will be helpful to move from a consideration of the social dimension of experience of God to explore the mystical side of our union with God. The need for such a "mystical" theology is apparent from the following story, which seems to me to be not at all unusual. A working mother had the chance to leave her children with some friends and to attend a weekend retreat. The retreat was silent, with long spaces which the retreatants could use for prayer and reflection if they so wanted. At the end of the first day the woman sought out the retreat director and asked for help. She said she could not pray. She had tried various prayer exercises and had tried to say as many vocal prayers as she could remember. It all left her feeling distracted and miserable. She said that this was always the way when she tried to pray.

The retreat director asked if she ever just spent some time with God. She replied that she did this often, and then she went on to describe how she had developed the habit of visiting a church after work and sitting there for a little while. She said: "I don't try to pray. I just sit there with God. When I come out I feel different. I feel as though I have been held."

The woman was relieved and greatly consoled when she was told that what she had been doing in the church was indeed prayer and a special gift from God, and that there was nothing to be gained by forcing herself to pray another way. There are many people, it seems to me, in a situation something like that of this woman. For the sake of such people it is important to attempt to clarify the way in which a person can be led by God to a mystical or contemplative mode of prayer.

Words like "mysticism," "contemplation" and "meditation" have different meanings for different people. Here I will use the words in what seems to me to be their traditional sense. Mystical experience then refers to those moments when prayer goes beyond thoughts and images, and becomes an experience of loving union with God. It refers to moments as ordinary and as profound as those that the woman in the story spent in the church. Such an experience may also be called "contemplative prayer." "Mystical prayer" and "contemplative prayer" refer to the same experience. They can both be clearly distinguished from meditation, which is a kind of prayer in which the intellect and the imagination have a large role.

In this chapter I follow John of the Cross in discussing the mystical side of experience of God under the symbol "dark night."[1] The symbol suggests two aspects of our experience of God. First, it is a dark night because we are called into a way of prayer which goes beyond thoughts and images to a union with God in darkness; in this context it will be helpful to discuss the movement from meditation to contemplation, and to consider the appropriate stance of a person called to a contemplative mode of prayer. Second, the symbol of the night suggests that contemplative union can occur in the darkness of suffering, and the experience of extreme dryness and emptiness in the life of faith. The chapter will conclude with some remarks about the connection and the difference between everyday experience of God and mystical experience.

The Dark Night: Pre-Conceptual Experience of God

John of the Cross draws upon a long tradition in his use of the image of darkness as a way of expressing a pre-conceptual union with God. St. Gregory of Nyssa, for example, writing in the fourth century, insists that we can come to union with God only in darkness. He chooses the image of darkness because it speaks of what is unknown and unseen. Commenting on Moses' experience of God on Mount Sinai, he reflects on the fact that Moses can encounter God only by approaching the dark cloud where God is.[2] For Gregory the lesson is that God "has made darkness his hiding place," and this means that we can approach God only in darkness, without intellectual comprehension. He speaks of the individual's journey toward God:

> For leaving behind everything that is observed, not only what sense comprehends but also what the intelligence thinks it sees, it keeps on penetrating deeper until by the intelligence's yearning for understanding it gains access to the invisible and the incomprehensible, and there it sees God. This is the true knowledge of what is sought, this is the seeing that consists in not seeing, because that which is sought transcends all knowledge, being separated on all sides by incomprehensibility as by a kind of darkness. Wherefore John the Sublime, who penetrated into the luminous darkness, says, "No one has ever seen God," thus asserting that knowledge of the divine essence is unattainable not only by men but also by every intelligent creature.[3]

These themes—that we can have access to God, but that this God remains invisible and incomprehensible, that the experience of God can be described both as luminous and as dark, that it is a seeing which is not seeing and a knowing in unknowing—remain constant in the Christian mystical tradition. In the East they form the basis of the negative (apophatic) stream of

Christian theology. The image of the dark cloud (from the story of Moses in Exodus 21 and from Psalm 17) becomes a favorite symbol for Christian spiritual writers.

The theme of darkness, so well developed by Gregory of Nyssa, is picked up by a fifth century monk who is often called Pseudo-Dionysius, since he writes under the pseudonym of Dionysius, a convert of St. Paul.

He describes a contemplation which goes beyond the senses and the activity of the intellect, and which goes in "unknowing" toward what he calls the "Ray of Divine Darkness."[4] In this kind of prayer the initiate is plunged into the darkness of unknowing and "through the passive stillness of all his reasoning powers" is united to "him that is wholly unknowable." This darkness, Dionysius writes, is not a negative darkness, but a "darkness beyond light."[5]

The teaching of Dionysius influences the whole Western tradition in the Middle Ages, including the great Scholastics. Thomas Aquinas treats these writings with great respect, believing them to be close to St. Paul and that therefore they have almost apostolic authority. In England *The Cloud of Unknowing* is a beautiful development of the themes of Gregory and Dionysius, and in northern Europe Eckhardt and Ruysbroeck build on the long apophatic tradition. In Spain the image of darkness becomes central to the thought of John of the Cross and in his writing it emerges as the symbol of dark night.

Out of the tradition of Christian spirituality and its insistence that our union with God takes place only in the darkness of unknowing, and out of his own experience of God and that of the people he directs, John of the Cross forges the symbol "dark night." Like all great symbols it emerges out of experience by a kind of inner necessity. Such symbols ought not be seen as logical constructs of the intellect, but rather as the direct expression in image of what is experienced.[6] Jean Baruzi, one of the great commentators of John of the Cross, has said of the symbol "dark night": "By a prodigy of the mystical imagination, the night is at one and the same time the most intimate translation of the experience and the experience itself."[7]

This dark night is the experience of contemplation. John of the Cross tells us that the individual, who comes to contemplation after being used to meditation, may find only dryness and distaste, since he or she is still accustomed to a way of experiencing which depends upon the senses, the imagination and the intellect. He comments on the soul experiencing the distaste: because "its spiritual palate is neither purged nor accommodated for so subtle a taste, it is unable to experience the spiritual savor and good until gradually prepared by means of this dark and obscure night."[8] God no longer communicates himself by means of "discursive analysis" and "synthesis of ideas," but "begins to communicate himself through pure spirit by an act of simple contemplation, in which there is not succession of thought."[9] Clearly it is a dark experience because it occurs at a pre-conceptual level.

As the long Christian mystical tradition asserts, contemplation is a union in love, a "loving knowledge," a knowing in unknowing. It is a union with God which transcends our conceptual knowledge. The intellect is in darkness, since God always remains incomprehensible to the human intellect. However mystics remain human and the human person needs to reflect on experience, even if the experience is unspeakable. When John of the Cross, one of the great poets of Spain, reflects on contemplative union, he expresses this union in the image "dark night." Because of his extraordinary imaginative powers he can find an image to express an experience of that which is inexpressible in itself. The magic of the symbol is that it does provide a way of speaking of an experience which cannot adequately be expressed, and at the same time the force of the image asserts that the experience is incomprehensible. It is rare that an image has such power to project us toward a reality which is beyond comprehension and imagination. It is, perhaps, the only image that can point so successfully to what cannot be imagined.

The symbol "dark night," of course, not only refers to the pre-conceptual mode of experience, but it points also to the content of the experience. The dark night is the inflow of God.[10] It is not that the night is preliminary to our encounter with God, but rather that it expresses the very reality we encounter. God himself comes to us as dark night. He is a dark night to us, experienced sometimes as the darkness of midnight, sometimes as "the tranquil night at the time of the rising dawn,"[11] but never as broad daylight, at least in this life. The symbol has the advantage of allowing us to speak of an awareness of God, while at the same time maintaining God's transcendence.

It is important to notice that this kind of union with God is not a rare thing, according to John of the Cross. It is not abnormal for people of prayer to receive the call to contemplation: "Not much time ordinarily passes after the initial stages of the spiritual life before beginners start to enter this night of sense."[12] At the same time it must be remembered that John of the Cross presumes that these "beginners" are practicing the Christian life with generosity, and this includes the asceticism outlined in *The Ascent of Mount Carmel*.

From Meditation to Contemplation

The classic treatment of meditation and contemplation, and of the movement from one to the other, is offered by John of the Cross. He is able to absorb the earlier mystical tradition and create his own synthesis with originality and clarity. He treats the matter explicitly in both *The Ascent of Mount Carmel* and *The Dark Night*.[13]

Meditation is a kind of prayer which depends upon the faculties of intellect and imagination. When we think about a

Scripture passage and reflectively apply it to our lives, then this is meditation. When we imagine a scriptural scene, and perhaps place ourselves in the situation so that, for example, we stand in imagination at the foot of the cross, then this kind of prayer is meditation. Meditation is a prayer which depends upon intellectual concepts, images and words.

Meditation, then, is our ordinary way of praying. It would be a great mistake to underrate its importance. This mistake is made at times because in the writings of John of the Cross and others meditation is distinguished from contemplation, and contemplation is certainly seen as a higher form of prayer. However for many of us, perhaps all of us, the two forms of prayer are both part of our normal pattern of relationship with God. There are times when meditative prayer is appropriate for all of us. Very often contemplative moments of prayer occur in prayer which has begun through the use of ideas, images or words. John of the Cross makes the point that even after God has drawn us to a contemplative mode of prayer we will very often need to return to meditation.[14]

In an important sense it is true that meditation is the essential foundation of all Christian prayer. Everything else depends upon the real listening to the word of God, and this means saturating ourselves with the words and deeds of Jesus as they are given to us in the Gospels. It means absorbing Jesus Christ with all our faculties. It means not only hearing the word and allowing it to echo deep within our beings, but it might also mean that we use our imagination to situate ourselves in a Gospel passage, or that we "mull over" the word, that we think about the word, connecting it with our lived experience. In this sense meditation, and meditative reading of the Gospels, not only will be the foundation of our prayer but it will be a constant necessity.

St. Ignatius in his *Spiritual Exercises* directs us to prayer exercises which he calls "contemplations."[15] They all depend upon a creative use of the imagination. It seems that he is using the word "contemplation" for what others would call "meditation." However Ignatius' contemplations are designed to lead to moments of union with God that will profoundly change lives. He invites retreatants to begin in the imagination precisely so that they may be led to a seeing and a tasting of what is beyond images and concepts. The fact that so many men and women have been led to a profound mystical prayer through this method of praying should be enough to stop us from setting up a false dichotomy between meditation using concepts and images and contemplation. Contemplation depends upon meditation, and contemplative moments often occur precisely within meditative prayer.

However, St. John of the Cross is concerned with another problem. He meets many men and women who have a distaste for their old way of praying and who find in themselves a desire to be in God's presence very quietly. Some of these people have spiritual directors who think they are lazy and who insist that they go back and pray in the old way. With others the problem comes from themselves: they think that if they stay before the Lord quietly without doing anything much they will be wasting time. John of the Cross feels a special mission to such people. He wants to liberate them for a whole new way of prayer. Such a liberation can occur, in his view, only when the Holy Spirit is drawing these persons to contemplation. However the question remains: How can a person know when God is inviting him or her to contemplative prayer? After studying the traditional literature on prayer and listening to the experience of countless men and women, lay people as well as his Carmelite brothers and sisters, John of the Cross comes to the conclusion that there are three signs which enable a person to know that he or she is called to contemplation.

The first sign is simply that a person can no longer meditate.[16] Meditative prayer, or the attempt to pray meditatively, leads only to an experience of extreme aridity.

The second sign is that a person has no desire to fix his or her attention upon some object apart from God. Such a person not only cannot meditate on what is of God, but also has no attraction to other things. If a person's waking hours are filled with some new project, then it could be this that makes meditation impossible. Of course distractions are always to be expected in the life of prayer, and John of the Cross is not talking about ordinary distractions. He is simply suggesting that if some person or object other than God is the focus of our attention, then this could well be the explanation for our inability to pray meditatively.

The most important sign is the third one: the person is inclined to remain in loving awareness of God, quietly and peacefully. There is no interest in thinking about, imagining or remembering particular things. Rather there is a preference for remaining in general, loving awareness of God.

These three signs provide us with clear guidelines. However in practice it is often not at all easy to know what is happening at such a time. For one thing the movement toward contemplation may be occurring in a time of intense darkness and confusion. It is always a time of reorientation. There is usually the pain of letting go of familiar patterns of prayer. However, the pain is the pain of birth; its fruit is illumination and liberation.

It is a confusing time for another reason—this pre-conceptual experience of God may not be recognized for what it is. For a person not used to contemplative prayer the experience of this loving knowledge is so subtle and delicate as to be almost imperceptible. A person used to thought and imagination in prayer may not recognize this gentle, subtle awareness as a genuine form of prayer.[17] It may be mistaken for fantasy or laziness.

This situation is a delicate one for the individual. It is a time when a person may need the help of an experienced spiritual director. Apparently in sixteenth century Spain there were many spiritual directors who were unable to recognize this moment of growth and of call. They were forcing their directees to persist in the attempt to meditate. There is real anger in the comments that John of the Cross makes on this kind of spiritual direction.[18] He is passionately concerned that individuals be helped to understand what their response should be when they were being called beyond meditation to contemplation.

The Stance of the Individual Called to Contemplation

What stance should a person take when he or she feels a repugnance to meditation, when there is no obvious external cause for this in the person's life, and when the person feels drawn to a prayer of quiet, loving awareness of God? In one of his most characteristic teachings John of the Cross urges the individual to follow the instinctive, deep response of his or her heart and to remain before the Lord quietly and peacefully.

He insists that the worst thing to do is to force oneself to pray in a way that has become repugnant. He acknowledges that many people, used to thoughts and images in prayer, may feel uncomfortable because they are not doing anything. Because of the conditioning of their earlier prayer life such people are tempted to think they have taken a wrong turn and are simply wasting time.

In the passage from *The Ascent of Mount Carmel* John of the Cross puts the matter very clearly:

> When the spiritual person cannot meditate, he should learn to remain in God's presence with a loving attention and a tranquil intellect, even though he seems to himself to be idle. For little by little and very soon the divine calm and

peace with a wondrous, sublime knowledge of God enveloped in divine love, will be infused into his soul. He should not interfere with forms of discursive meditations and imaginings. Otherwise his soul will be disquieted and drawn out of its peaceful contentment to distaste and repugnance. And if, as we said, scruples about his inactivity arise, he should remember that pacification of soul (making it calm and peaceful, inactive and desireless) is no small accomplishment.[19]

There is a very similar passage in *The Dark Night,* and here John of the Cross speaks of remaining in "rest and quiet" and of "a loving and peaceful attentiveness to God."[20] He encourages the person to freedom in this new experience. The task of the spiritual director is to encourage the individual to persevere patiently, to be quiet and peaceful, and simply to turn to God with loving attention.

This stance of the individual is to a large extent a receptive one. Words that characterize this response are "quietness," "stillness," "emptiness" and "receptivity." However there is an active dimension in the individual's response. The person is called to an active waiting and listening and attending. It is an active receptivity.

These attitudes are, of course, precisely the ones that allow an individual to dwell in an experience that is pre-conceptual. They are the attitudes by which a person can remain in a moment of loving encounter without the meditations of concepts or images.

In the years since John of the Cross other writers have spoken of this human stance as "acquired contemplation" or "active contemplation." However in the writing of John of the Cross the word "contemplation" is used to refer to the inflow of God; it is a gift that is received by the person passively. His own phrase, in the passage quoted above, describes the human stance well: "He should learn to remain in God's presence with loving attention and a tranquil intellect." This suggests that the human stance before the gift of God that is contemplative experience might well be described as the prayer of loving attention.

These reflections have been concerned with the pre-conceptual nature of contemplative experience, and with the movement from meditation to this kind of prayer. This movement in itself is a kind of purification. Although it is beyond the scope of this book to consider it in detail, it is important to discuss the deeper purification that may accompany contemplative experience, the painful sense of aridity and abandonment.

The Dark Night: Aridity and Abandonment

In his book, *The Dark Night,* John of the Cross explains how contemplation, which is always God's gift and which the soul always receives passively, purifies the soul. He speaks of the night of sense and the night of spirit. In the night of sense a person is led to an initial purification. At the core of this is the movement in prayer from meditation to contemplation, which has already been discussed. This initial purification may take place within an experience of great aridity. It is usually followed by a time of peace and consolation as a person enjoys the new freedom of contemplative prayer. However the person may be led, after a while, to a new and much more painful experience of dryness and isolation from God that John of the Cross calls the dark night of spirit.

What is this dark night like? What kind of experience is John of the Cross addressing? A woman who has been faithful to prayer for many years may find herself filled with a sense of herself as unworthy and sinful. This may become so acute that she feels that she has effectively cut herself off from God's love.

She can see no way that God could associate himself with a person as wretched as herself. A man may find himself unable to pray in any way which brings him a sense of satisfaction. His prayer becomes painfully arid. God seems remote. Such a man may feel totally abandoned by God. He may also feel isolated from his friends. All he can do is cry out with Jesus on the cross: "My God, my God, why have you abandoned me?" Even belief in God may begin to seem impossible, and faith, then, is something to which he can cling only in total darkness. When such persons are offered comfort by a friend or a spiritual director, they may be unable to receive the well-intentioned words of encouragement. A person in this dark night may feel that others simply do not understand what it is like to feel so hopelessly miserable, or to experience an unbridgeable chasm opened up between God and self. There appears to be no possibility of relief from the kind of aridity and loneliness they are experiencing.

If this seems to be rather a grim picture, it is not nearly as grim or as detailed as the description that John of the Cross offers. It seems that he is determined to present a picture of the worst possible misery and suffering a person may have, in order that anyone who is in this dark night may recognize that his or her suffering, no matter how great it seems, is really a movement of purification. No matter how bleak the experience, it is part of a positive movement. The whole point is to affirm that the deepest human suffering, including the sufferings connected with the struggle for faith, not only do not distance us from God but must actually be seen as a moment of intense union with God: this "dark night is an inflow of God into the soul which purges it of its habitual ignorances and imperfections, natural and spiritual, and which contemplatives call infused contemplation or mystical theology."[21]

The reason for the pain of this night is reducible to the

philosophical principle which states that two contraries cannot exist in the same subject. It is not that this contemplative faith is a harsh and difficult reality in itself. On the contrary, "the light and the wisdom of this contemplation is very bright and pure,"[22] and the pain and discordance comes from our own spiritual misery, wretchedness and sin that cannot receive this divinizing life without a painful transformation. St. John comments: "How amazing and pitiful it is that the soul be so utterly weak and impure that the hand of God, though light and gentle, should feel so heavy and contrary."[23] A little later he returns to this theme:

> There is nothing in contemplation or the divine inflow which of itself can give pain; contemplation rather bestows sweetness and delight. The cause for not experiencing these agreeable effects is the soul's weakness and imperfection at that time, its inadequate preparation, and the qualities it possesses which are contrary to this light.[24]

The pain of the dark night is the pain of radical transformation. A person is being led into a union with the divine. For this work of divinization to occur, the roots of evil that reach into the core of the human person must be plucked out. The dark night is, then, a night of liberation.

Although this night darkens the spirit, it does so that light may come: "In the midst of those dark and loving afflictions, the soul feels the presence of someone and an interior strength."[25] The person will come again to experience the enkindling of love and the illumination of a new, delightful and delicate awareness of the beloved. In this enkindling there is a "certain touch of the divinity," a touch of a sublime "experience and love of God."[26]

It must be remembered that for John of the Cross the dark night is not ultimately a wretched and miserable experience.

Rather it is a night to be celebrated, as it is in the greatest of St. John's poems:

> O guiding night!
> O night more lovely than the dawn!
> O night that has united
> The Lover with His beloved,
> Transforming the beloved in her
> Lover.[27]

The Relationship Between "Everyday" Experience of God and Mystical Experience

If there are experiences of God which occur in our day to day lives, experiences like the moments of abundant richness and of limitation described in an earlier chapter, and there is also the experience of God in contemplative prayer described in this chapter, then a further question arises about the connection between these two experiences. How is contemplative prayer related to the experiences of God that occur in daily life? Is there continuity between the two experiences so that contemplative prayer is simply a more intense form of the everyday experience of God? Can an "ordinary" experience of God, such as the experience of God's presence in the beauty of nature, become contemplative prayer?

These questions can be answered by attending carefully to the nature of the two experiences. The experience of God occurs as we live out our lives in the world. It occurs in and through such an event as our love for a friend. In our knowledge and love of our friend the object of our attention is this friend. Our conceptual awareness and our love is directed toward this specific person. However in and through our focus on this one person there can arise a sense of mystery and of God's presence at the heart of the relationship. To return to the image that was used in earlier chapters the experience of God can occur as the horizon to our experience of a friend.

How is contemplative experience different from this? In contemplation as John of the Cross describes it, the person abandons concepts and images and remains before God in the darkness of faith and the stance of loving attention. It is an experience of the presence of God and the intimate union with him which occurs without the use of concepts or images.

This suggests a way of understanding the connection and the difference between everyday experience of God and mystical experience. In this everyday experience of God an object in the world, such as a friend, is the center of conscious attention while the mystery of God is experienced in a pre-conceptual way as horizon to this experience of a friend. In mysticism the mystery of God is the center of conscious attention and love, without however being reduced to concepts or images. In everyday experience of grace God is experienced as horizon and ground to another experience, while in contemplation God himself is at the center. This means that there is real continuity between the two experiences, but there is more than a difference of degree between them. The distinction is made on the basis of the question as to whether God is experienced as center or as subsidiary to some other worldly experience. In both instances, of course, experience of God occurs at a pre-conceptual level.

Everyday experience of God can, then, become a moment of contemplation. The conceptual object of my attention (such as the beauty of the sunrise) can begin to become transparent, and the mystery of God, which at first was experienced only as horizon, may begin to become the center of attention and love. When the everyday experience, in which the experience of grace occurs, begins to fade as the focus of intellect and will, and grace itself becomes the center, then the experience of grace has become a moment of contemplation.[28]

This distinction also helps explain how meditation can become contemplation.[29] As a person meditates on a scene from the life of Christ, then the focus of conceptual awareness may well be the concrete event as it is recreated in the person's imagination. However in this meditation there may arise also a sense of mystery of God's presence and love, which is experienced in a pre-conceptual way. A person, in this situation, might feel drawn to dwell in this sense of God's loving presence. In this case the image becomes transparent to the reality. The person no longer imagines the scene or thinks out his or her responses, or at least these activities are not the focus of attention; rather the individual is drawn to dwell pre-conceptually on the mystery of God, and this mystery is the center of the person's conscious attention and love.

eight

FINDING GOD'S WILL

The Church has a great tradition of moral teaching and moral theology which can act as a major signpost for Christian decision-making. However there are many decisions which a Christian may be called upon to make which neither the Gospels nor the moral tradition of the Church illuminates in any direct way: a young couple setting up their own home may have to decide to what extent, and in what ways, their lifestyle will reflect alternative values to their culture's materialism; a mother may need to decide whether to take on a job or whether to put all her creative energy into her home and her involvement in community activities; a man may have to wrestle with a decision whether or not he will accept more responsibility at work when this option will mean that there is less time and energy to give to family life; a man or woman, whose life already seems full, may need to decide whether to take on one more activity, be it involvement in a social issue or work on a committee of the parish. Many decisions, whether they be as big as the choice of vocation in life, or as small as a choice about the time a person rises in the morning, are well beyond the scope of Christian moral teaching.

Yet a Christian who seeks to follow Jesus will place great priority on doing the will of God in all things. Is there any way, beyond the ethical teaching of the Scriptures and of the Church, that God's will can be found in the ordinary areas of life? In this chapter I will be suggesting that there is such a way of seeking to find God's will, and that it is directly related to our experience of God. To this end it will be helpful to consider four original thinkers in this area: Paul, Thomas Aquinas, Ignatius Loyola and Karl Rahner.

Discernment of Spirits in Paul

It is not unusual for us to find ourselves drawn in different directions by a variety of influences. These influences include the expressed wishes of people we love, the advice of those we trust, the need to provide responsibly for family life, the demands made upon us in our workplace, the effect of advertising and the pressure to conform to the expectations of our society and our peer groups. This list could be extended almost endlessly. Sometimes competing external pressures pull us in directions that are quite contradictory, and, for example, a man or woman may be tugged in one direction by the expectations of work life and in the opposite direction by the needs of home life.

We also experience a variety of inner impulses. Arising from within there are attractions, resistances, hungers, fears, hopes and doubts. There is the experience of restlessness and the experience of inner peace. A proposed decision may arouse conflicting movements within a person. The same course of action may be appealing and challenging, and yet at the same time it may arouse obscure fears that cannot be quite understood.

The biblical authors were quite aware of this problem. They tended to speak of these various pulls that we experience as coming from different "spirits." Among the gifts of the Holy Spirit St. Paul lists "the ability to distinguish between spirits" (1 Cor 12:10). From then on "discernment of spirits" becomes a key issue in Christian spirituality. In 1 John we read: "Beloved, do not believe every spirit, but test the spirits to see whether they are of God" (4:1).

If we are to find God's will in our lives, it is obvious that we must come to know which promptings are of God and which are not. We must test the spirits, as the author of 1 John tells us. But how can we carry out this test? What are our criteria for discernment of spirits? How can we find God's will in our lives?

It goes without saying that we must use all the ordinary means at our disposal in coming to a decision. This means making an intellectual assessment of the positive and negative values in a decision, taking into account any authoritative teaching on the issue at hand, and taking appropriate advice.

We often do all these things and still find that the direction is not clear. Is there any further means of discovering what is of God and what is not? St. Paul offers us some helpful criteria.[1] First he tells us that we can recognize the good and bad spirits by their fruits. The fruits of the bad spirit (the "flesh") are "immorality, impurity, licentiousness, idolatry, sorcery, enmity, strife, jealousy, anger, selfishness, dissensions, party spirit, envy, drunkenness, carousing and the like." The fruits of the Holy Spirit are "love, joy, peace, patience, kindness, goodness, faithfulness, gentleness, self control" (Gal 5:19–23). What is of God's Spirit in our lives should result in our experience of these fruits of the Spirit.

A second criteria for Paul has to do with the Church. That which builds up the community is likely to be of God. This is the whole argument of 1 Corinthians 12—14. Everything is tested against the good of the whole Church. Charismatic gifts are significant only in this context. Paul writes bluntly: "Since you are eager for manifestations of the Spirit, strive to excel in building up the church" (1 Cor 14:12).

Love is a third criterion for Paul. All spiritual gifts are ordered to love, and any so-called spiritual gifts that do not lead to love are not of God. Love is the supreme norm:

> If I speak in the tongues of men and of angels, but have not love, I am a noisy gong or a clanging symbol. And if I have prophetic powers, and understand all mysteries and all knowledge, and if I have all faith, so as to remove mountains but have not love, I am nothing. If I give away all I have, and if I deliver my body to be burned, but have not love, I gain nothing (1 Cor 13:1–3).

Fourth, he tells us that a basic criterion concerns a person's relationship to the Lord Jesus: that which leads to a confession of the Lordship of Jesus is of God (1 Cor 12:3), and that which leads away from Jesus is not of God. In 1 John we find this same criterion expressed: "You can tell the spirits that come from God by this: every spirit which acknowledges that Jesus the Christ has come in the flesh is from God, but any spirit which will not say this of Jesus is not of God" (4:2–3).

These four criteria provide an initial basis for discernment. Paul also speaks in terms of signs of power which accompany the preaching of the Gospel (1 Thess 1:4–6) and of his own revelation and experience of the risen Lord. This experience linked him with the apostles and authorized him in his mission. In some ways this experience of the Lord constitutes the fundamental test for everything in the life of Paul (Gal 1:16–17). As well as the normal criteria for distinguishing between spirits, then, there can be a clear revelation from God, a moment so incontestably "of God" that it can provide a framework and basis for all decisions.

St. Thomas and the Gift of Wisdom

There have been few thinkers who have been as consistently rational and logical in their development of an intellectual system as Thomas Aquinas. Yet we find in him a real integration of experience and theology. It is reported that he would read Cassian every day, and he is quoted as saying: "From this reading I reap devotion, and that makes it easier for me to lift myself up into speculation. So the *affectus,* attachment to God, widens into devotion, and, thanks to it, the intellect ascends toward the highest summits."[2] In 1273 after a mystical experience during his celebration of the Eucharist he stopped work on his *Summa Theologiae,* telling his secretary: "All I have written seems to me like so much straw compared with what I have seen and with what has been revealed to me."[3]

Thomas develops a finely tuned moral theology that is built upon a logical and scientific approach to ethical questions. However alongside this rational approach, which he obviously values, he outlines another approach to finding God's will—the way of "connaturality."

Thomas follows Augustine's teaching that there is a Trinitarian "mission" to the individual person. The Spirit and the Son are sent to us, Augustine writes, and if they are sent to us then we must be able to "perceive" them.[4] He is unable to conceive of a mission that is not perceptible. Thomas, commenting on Augustine, tells us that the word "perception" points to a kind of "experiential awareness" of the presence of the Holy Spirit and the Word.[5] Thomas asks himself how these persons of the Trinity are experienced. He answers that, since the Holy Spirit is love, when the Spirit is sent to a person the Spirit is perceived in the gift of love, a gift by which the soul is likened to the Holy Spirit.[6] But what of the Word? Thomas answers that the Son is the "Word breathing love," and so "not just any enhancing of the mind indicates the Son's being sent, but only that sort of enlightening that bursts forth into love."[7] We become aware of the Spirit as a movement of love, and we become aware of the Word as enlightenment accompanied by love.

The indwelling of God is not something that we can perceive with the knowledge of rational comprehension. Rather it is a knowing through love, a loving knowledge. St. Thomas tells us that such loving knowledge is a gift of the Holy Spirit: it is the gift of wisdom.[8] Using a play on words, Thomas tells us that wisdom (sapientia) is a knowledge that is tasted (sapida).[9] This wisdom, this taste for what is of God, is the virtue and the gift by which we can be enabled to make a wise decision, a decision that is faithful to God's will.

Thomas explains the matter by way of an example. There are two ways, he tells us, that a person can come to make a decision about what is chaste conduct. One way is through the careful applications of rational moral principles to a particular case. However, there is also another way. A person who has the virtue of chastity may make the right choice through a kind of connaturality with what is good and chaste.[10] A chaste person has a kind of natural at-homeness with chastity that enables him or her to choose rightly. This kind of "instinctive affinity" or "at-homeness" is what St. Thomas means by connaturality.

By virtue of this connaturality a person can make a judgment about what is of God. Wisdom, the gift of the Holy Spirit, enables us to judge rightly about what is of God because of a kind of instinctive affinity (connaturality) for the things that are of God. This affinity for divine things results from the love by which we are bound to God.[11]

Because God has united himself radically to us, because we have a kind of loving awareness of God present in our hearts through the gift of wisdom, we are enabled to make right judgments because of an instinctive oneness with what is of God.

This teaching of St. Thomas makes it clear that while our discernment of God's will can occur simply through a use of intellectual argument, there is another way of knowing what is of God, the way of connaturality. This second way is built upon an experience of God. It tests a concrete choice against what is "tasted" of God. This concept, under a different name, is central in the theory of discernment outlined by St. Ignatius of Loyola.

St. Ignatius and the "Consolation Without Cause"

For Ignatius the whole process of finding God's will and following it is a central theme. He quite unambiguously believes that God has a unique will for each of us, that he does communicate his will to us in a personal way and that we can learn to hear this word that is spoken to us.

The central text of St. Ignatius is the *Spiritual Exercises,* a book which is geared toward a retreat experience. However the retreat experience is one in which the retreatant is called to a radical conversion, and this conversion is to be lived out in the events of the person's daily life. At the heart of the *Spiritual Exercises* is the assumption that a person will be making a choice about a way of life. The *Exercises* are concerned with discovering God's will in the reality of everyday life.

The candidate for the *Spiritual Exercises* must allow for the possibility that God's will may be communicated in a personal way. How can such a person come to know God's will? Ignatius speaks of three "times" when we can come to know the will of God.[12]

The first time is through a clear and explicit call from God. We are so moved by God that we cannot doubt the call and, like Paul on the road to Damascus, we are moved to follow an unmistakable invitation. The second time is through the movements of spirits and the discernment of these spirits. In this second time light and knowledge of God's will can be attained through the experience of what Ignatius calls consolations and desolations. The third time is through a rational choice, a clearheaded intellectual assessment of the values involved. Ignatius presents two exercises for such a rational evaluation.[13]

What is really interesting is that St. Ignatius presents this rational approach last and says that it is to be used when there is no movement of spirits and when election has not been made in the first or second way. It seems as though the rational approach is a kind of last resort. Even when we make a decision in this way Ignatius insists that we must take it to prayer and ask the Lord to confirm it.[14] This confirmation can occur only through a movement of spirits similar to the first or second time. All of this is saying that Ignatius believed that the movement of spirits (the "second time") and the clear call of God (the "first time") are the privileged ways of coming to know God's will.

Of course it may well happen that all three ways, or "times," are part of one single process of discernment of God's will.[15] They cannot be completely separated from one another. However if the first "time" is the time of exceptional clarity about God's call and the third "time" is the last resort, then this suggests that the normal pattern of finding God's will is the way of the second "time," the movements of consolation and desolation and the discernment of spirits.

What are these "consolations" and "desolations"? According to Ignatius consolations are interior movements of the soul such as these: "when an interior movement is aroused in the soul, by which it is enflamed with love of its Creator and Lord, and, as a consequence, can love no creature on the face of the earth for its own sake, but only in the Creator of them all"; "when one sheds tears that move to the love of God, whether it be because of sorrow for sins, or because of the sufferings of Christ our Lord, or for any other reason that is immediately directed to the praise and service of God"; "every increase of faith, hope and love, and all interior joy that invites and attracts to what is heavenly and to the salvation of one's soul by filling it with peace and quiet in its Creator and Lord."[16]

Desolation, Ignatius tells us, involves the opposite kinds of movements: "darkness of soul, turmoil of spirit, inclination to what is low and earthly, restlessness rising from any disturbances and temptations, which lead to want of faith, want of hope, want of love."[17] In desolation the soul is "wholly slothful, tepid, sad and separated, as it were, from its Creator and Lord."[18]

Desolation may occur for different reasons. It may be the result of our own infidelity, or it may be a time of trial, or it may be a time when the Lord leaves us to ourselves in order that we may more truly know ourselves and that consolation is God's gift.[19] Consolation, too, can have several causes. It may come, Ignatius tells us, from the good angel or from the evil spirit.[20] The experience of consolations and desolations cannot be used simplistically to determine what is of the good or bad spirit. Ignatius gives many wise and finely tuned directions for the discernment of such spirits.

For example he shows that when a soul is progressing toward perfection, the promptings of the good spirit will be gentle and delightful, while the evil spirit acts upon the soul in ways that are "violent, noisy and disturbing."[21] However, when the soul is going from bad to worse, then the good spirit will appear as disruptive and desolating, while the evil spirit's promptings will appear as agreeable and consoling.

The directions that Ignatius gives are too subtle to summarize here. They depend upon their whole context in the *Spiritual Exercises*. What is important for our purposes is that Ignatius asserts that we can reflect upon our own experience of the movement of spirits, and from that reflection we can come to know what leads to good and what leads to evil.[22]

It is important to emphasize that for Ignatius a retreatant learns discernment within a process which involves growing freedom from disordered attachments and a progressive identification with the mind and heart of Jesus Christ. Important decisions should be made only when a person has found a certain amount of freedom. This freedom (or "indifference") is attained only when a person recognizes and accepts that, in a decision involving a choice between two directions, God might be leading in either direction. What seems least attractive might well be of God. This kind of freedom comes from prayerful confrontation with Jesus in the Gospels: with his constant surrender to the Father's will, his acceptance of the collapse of his own project and of the way of the cross. A real identification with Jesus creates the possibility of going beyond attachment to one direction, to a real openness and freedom to accept that God's will might lead in either direction. The way of the Lord may well include a call to the cross.

Ignatius offers us further help in finding God's will. He believes that there are certain psychological impulses that can be recognized as coming from God. These are what he calls "consolations without previous cause." When we experience this kind of consolation it is not caused by good or bad spirits but only by God. Such an experience can provide a solid basis for knowing what is "of God," for finding God's will.

Ignatius speaks of this kind of consolation in two of the Rules for the Discernment of Spirits (the second and eighth rules):

> God alone can give consolation to the soul without any previous cause. It belongs solely to the Creator to come into the soul, to leave it, to act upon it, to draw it wholly to the love of His Divine Majesty. I said without previous cause, that is, without any preceding perception or knowledge of any subject by which a soul might be led to such a consolation through its own acts of intellect and will.

> When consolation is without previous cause, as was said, there can be no deception in it, since it can proceed from God our Lord alone. But a spiritual person who has received such a consolation must consider it very attentively, and must cautiously distinguish the actual time of the consolation from the period which follows it. At such a time the

soul is still fervent and favored with the grace and the after-
effects of the consolation which has passed. In the second
period the soul frequently forms various resolutions and
plans which are not granted directly by God our Lord.
They may come from our own reasoning on the relations of
our concepts and the consequences of our judgments, they
may come from the good or evil spirit. Hence, they must be
carefully examined before they are given full approval and
put into execution.[23]

This kind of experience occurs when the Creator draws the
person wholly into love of the Divine. Here we find a consolation which can be the criterion for the movements of our hearts.
When something is clearly of God, then everything else in life
can be tested against it.

This suggests that an appropriate way of discovering God's
will is by way of testing a decision against this experience which
is so uniquely of God, the consolation without cause. If there is
this kind of consolation in our lives, and it is unambiguously of
God, then we have a basis for knowing God's will.

Two questions immediately present themselves. What exactly is this consolation without cause? How can we apply it to
our own search for God's will in our lives? These questions have
been addressed by Karl Rahner.

Finding God's Will—Karl Rahner

Rahner asks himself the question: What is the consolation
without cause of which Ignatius speaks? He answers that it is
precisely a pre-conceptual experience of God, the kind of experience that has been discussed in earlier chapters of this book.[24]
There is no created cause for our consolation. There is no intellectual, imaginative or external cause for what we experience.
Rather we simply find ourselves open to the mystery of God,

drawn into his love. It is a moment when our beings are open and receptive to God and there is no intermediary, no concept or image, between ourselves and God.

At its highest, then, it is a moment of contemplation. When we find ourselves called to a moment of union with God in love without the mediations of images, concepts and words, then we have a consolation without cause. This interpretation of Rahner's is confirmed by looking at Ignatius' eighth rule of discernment (quoted above). Once we have passed from the first state of consolation without previous cause (from the pre-conceptual experience of God) in which there is no deceit, to a second stage of reflection which involves "resolutions," "plans," "reasonings," "concepts" and "judgments," then again we may be deceived. Clearly Ignatius is distinguishing between an original pre-conceptual encounter and our interpretation of this encounter in our own consciousness.

Rahner suggests that our experience of grace in life can become just such an encounter. As has been seen already, a person who encounters God as the mystery of grace in the day to day events of life can begin to attend fully to this God present by grace. This day to day experience can become transparent so that we are focally (but pre-conceptually) aware of the mystery of God, and our hearts are taken in love of this mystery.[25] Such a moment would be an instance of the pure consolation of which St. Ignatius speaks. Moments of contemplation in prayer would also be instances of this kind of consolation.

The touchstone for discovering the will of God is precisely the experience of God as we have been discussing it: a pre-conceptual loving union with God, in which he is the center of our attention and love. The consolation is not something added on to this experience; rather it is simply the effect in us of the experience of grace. When our whole beings are open to this experience, the effect in us is that we actually experience the fruits of the spirit—peace, joy and tranquillity.[26]

If the pre-conceptual, loving encounter with God is the criterion for finding God's will, the next question is a practical one: How can we make decisions in the light of this experience? Rahner's answer is simple: God's will is discovered through an experimental test. A particular matter to be discerned is placed against a person's experience of God and kept there. Holding what one is about to decide against the experience of openness to God should reveal whether the particular matter in question is in harmony with what one experiences of God.[27] The synthesis of the proposed decision and our experience of God may produce peace and tranquillity or it may produce unease and lack of peace.

It is really a matter of testing whether what we might do is congruent or incongruent with our deepest sense of God. Avery Dulles has described the process quite simply: "Through a process of 'play acting' we imaginatively place ourselves in the situation we are on the point of choosing, attempting to measure whether it is translucent to pure consolation."[28]

Such an experimental test may need to take place over a long time. The choice that is made is not directly revealed by God. God reveals himself to us (obscurely) in the mystery of his grace. We make a decision in the light of our perception of congruence or incongruence between the matter being discerned and our experience of grace. Such congruence or lack of it may not be immediately evident.

This means, of course, that people who have never made the *Spiritual Exercises* can also make decisions in the light of their experience of grace in the way that St. Ignatius proposed. Rahner goes further than this and suggests that ordinary people who have never heard of Ignatius and his directions actually do make decisions in much the way that Ignatius was suggesting. Sometimes a person who has to make a decision will take a long time to "think the matter over."

However it seems that this is not purely a rational matter;

the decision is often made on the grounds of what seems to "suit" the individual, or what he or she is "at home with." The same process is revealed when a person expresses the need to "sleep on" a decision. Such a person, Rahner suggests, "will probably make his decision through a fundamental global awareness of himself actually present and making itself felt in him during this space and time, and through a feeling of harmony or disharmony of the object of choice with this fundamental feeling he has about himself."[29] Now part of this global sense of self is the whole dimension of mystery, or of God's presence in life. What is most truly and deeply in tune with self is in tune with grace. But, of course, grace may not be consciously noticed.

Ordinary people, then, instinctively make important decisions in what is essentially the same way that Ignatius outlines. As Aristotle discovered the rules of logic and made explicit what was already practiced by ordinary people, so Ignatius discovered the rules for making a decision (finding God's will) and made explicit what ordinary people often practice.[30] With Ignatius the process becomes refined and therefore more helpful for difficult vocational decisions.

This argument of Rahner's seems to me to be quite convincing. There is a real link between everyday decisions which are made in tune with the deepest sense of self and the process of finding God's will that is suggested by Ignatius. However, it is important to sound a note of warning here. There is much more room for self-delusion in everyday decisions (as when a person makes a decision on the basis of what he or she feels "at home with") since there is always the possibility that we are opting for something that is self-centered. The more refined process of Ignatius creates the possibility of real freedom to make the hard choice, and also seeks to ensure that we are testing a decision not against a superficial level of self, but against a real openness to the mystery of God.

A Process for Christian Decision-Making

It might be helpful, at this stage, to summarize what has been said about finding God's will by outlining a process for Christian decision-making.

1. Preparation
A. Pray for light and freedom to follow God's will.

B. Clarify the options for discernment. It might be helpful to list the "pros" and "cons" for both directions in which God might be leading. This intellectual assessment should then be left behind as a person moves more deeply into the process.

2. Finding Freedom
A. Recognize that God might be leading in either direction. Our own emotional attachment to one direction might come from an attachment to our *own* way, or to a refusal to face the cross in our lives.

B. Confront the Gospel of Jesus in Prayer. Reflective prayer over a Gospel text puts us in touch with the way of Jesus, his surrender to the Father, his acceptance of the collapse of his own project and his way of the cross. The Gospels call us to an active choice to follow Jesus and to the desire to share his stance before the Father. Taking on the mind of Christ in this way can free us to go beyond our conscious or unconscious attachments.

3. Making the Decision
A. Evoke and remember in prayer the most central and abiding experience of God in life, a time of openness to God in love, a time when God is experienced as calling into a complete "yes." Hold in prayer this experience of union with God.

B. Call to mind one of the directions in which God may be calling and place this alongside the central experience of God. Notice whether the union of the two produces a sense of congruence and deep peace, or incongruence and disharmony. Repeat with the other direction.

C. The direction of God's call will be indicated by the level of congruence that is experienced between the choice to be made and the experience of God. Notice that there is no special revelation or magic at work here, but rather our own assessment of congruence, which may take a long time.

4. Confirmation

A. A decision that is made needs to be confirmed after prayer time in the hours, days and weeks that follow. As we go about our daily duties and face difficulties in life, what is truly of God will find confirmation in a sense of deep peace in God, in spite of external complexities. The decision we have made will need to find confirmation in its actual effects. This means that the way it affects others, and what it opens up in us, will be experienced as of God.

B. In prayer we can place the matter again before our God and test it to ensure that it leads to peace and sits well with that part of our being where we are open to the Spirit.

nine

VISIONS, VOICES AND TONGUES

Men and women who take their prayer seriously will sometimes report "extraordinary" prayer experiences. These experiences may include visions, the hearing of voices, or speaking in tongues.

How are these religious phenomena to be assessed? Are they to be seen as due to the direct intervention of God? Are they, on the contrary, to be seen as simply the products of excited human psyches? How should we respond if these things occur in our own lives? What response should we make when another person claims to speak for God as a result of a vision?

Evaluating Visions, Voices and Tongues

John of the Cross has a fully developed discussion of most of the different kinds of religious phenomena that occur among people of prayer in his book *The Ascent of Mount Carmel*.[1] By and large his attitude is that while these experiences may be the result of God's action (according to him they may also be caused by the action of evil spirits or by the persons themselves), yet they are not to be emphasized, clung to or sought after. If they are of God, then it will be the inner action of God in the heart that will be the important thing, not the external manifestation.

The appropriate attitude is to turn from these experiences back to the best road to God, which is that of dark contemplative faith. One way to appreciate the position of John of the Cross is through a study of his treatment of those imaginative visions, which he describes as "supernatural." For John of the Cross this means experiences caused by a supernatural agent which might be God or which might be evil spirits. He teaches that both God and evil spirits can present images to our imagination. The difference is that God is not limited to this means of communicating to the soul, but dwells in the soul "substantially" and can communicate through deeper and more spiritual ways.

John of the Cross, then, believes that it is better not to even try to discern which visions are of God and which are not. He wants simply to stop people being harmed by paying attention to visions. False visions deceive the soul, but true visions (those that are of God) can also hinder and block the path to union with God. These two paragraphs from *The Ascent of Mount Carmel* put the matter quite clearly:

> I affirm, then, that since these imaginative apprehensions, visions, and other forms of species are presented through some image or particular idea, a person must neither feed upon nor encumber himself with them. And this is true whether these visions are false and diabolical or whether they are recognized as authentic and of divine origin. Neither should a person desire to accept them or keep them, because with such an attitude he cannot remain detached, divested, pure, and simple, and without any mode or method, as the union demands.
>
> The reason is that in being apprehended these forms are always represented as we said in some limited mode or manner. But God's wisdom to which the intellect must be united has neither mode nor manner, neither does it have limits nor does it pertain to distance and particular knowl-

edge, because it is totally pure and simple. That the two extremes, the soul and the divine wisdom, may be united, they will have to come to accord by means of a certain likeness. As a result the soul must also be pure and simple, unlimited and unattached to any particular knowledge, and unmodified by the boundaries of form, species, and image. Since God is unincluded in any image, form, or particular knowledge, the soul in order to be united with Him should not be limited to any particular form or knowledge.[2]

The reason for St. John's negative attitude is pastoral, but it depends upon a theological understanding. God is totally other than our images or concepts of him. John of the Cross believes that images and concepts are a remote means to union with God. They do lead us toward God, but such images and concepts are not God. There is a shorter and surer path to God (John of the Cross calls it "proportionate and proximate" means to union). This is the path of dark contemplative faith, discussed in these pages as pre-conceptual union with God.[3] The problem with visions is that they do not unite us directly to God (the image is not God) and they can distract us from what does take us directly to God, dark contemplative faith.

The only possible reason for admitting and valuing such visions, he tells us, is the profit that genuine visions might bring to the soul. However the good that God would do is through an interior communication of "knowledge, or love, or sweetness." This kind of communication happens directly through God's action.[4] What God wants to happen in the depths of the soul will happen even when the person adopts a negative approach to the imaginative visions. It is appropriate, then, to value and to be grateful for God's gifts given in the heart irrespective of whether they are accompanied by an imaginative vision. However the vision itself is not important, and not the best road of access to God. The image of the vision is too far distant from the reality of

God. The opposite is true of the path of dark faith—it leads to God without the mediations of images or concepts.

The experience of visions and voices can be of three kinds.[5] First, a person may have an experience in which it seems that something is seen or heard by means of the bodily senses. This is an experience of something external to the person and is sometimes called a "corporeal" vision. The second kind of vision is of the "imaginative" kind. This is an interior experience produced in the imagination. It is sometimes an experience of quite distinct images and interior words, which are recognized as occurring within the person. The third kind of vision or experience of words is more difficult to describe. It is often referred to as an "intellectual" experience. It is the perception of spiritual truth in an obscure way without clear images.

Evelyn Underhill writes of this third kind of experience: "The 'intellectual vision,' like the 'substantial word' as described to us by the mystics, is of so elusive, spiritual, and formless a kind that it is hard to distinguish it from that act of pure contemplation in which it often takes its rise."[6] The fact that it is so "formless" and so close to dark contemplation explains why the great mystical writers take these experiences much more seriously than the more external "corporeal" visions.[7] St. Teresa's vision of the Blessed Trinity is of this interior, "intellectual" kind,[8] as is the vision of Jesus which she describes in her *Life:*

After two years of all these prayers of mine and those of others offered for the said intention (that the Lord would either lead me by another way or make known the truth, for the locutions I mentioned that the Lord granted me were experienced very repeatedly), the following happened to me. Being in prayer on the feastday of the glorious St. Peter, I saw or, to put it better, I felt Christ beside me; I saw nothing with my bodily eyes or with my soul, but it seemed to me that Christ was at my side—I saw that it was He, in my opinion, who was speaking to me. Since I was completely unaware that there could be a vision like this one, it greatly frightened me in the beginning. I did nothing but weep. However, by speaking one word alone, to assure me, the Lord left me feeling as I usually did: quiet, favored, and without any fear. It seemed to me that Jesus Christ was always present at my side; but since this wasn't an imaginative vision, I didn't see any form. Yet I felt very clearly that He was always present at my right side and that He was the witness of everything I did. At no time in which I was a little recollected, or not greatly distracted, was I able to ignore that He was present at my side.

I immediately went very anxiously to my confessor to tell him. He asked me in what form I saw Him. I answered that I didn't see Him. He asked how I knew that it was Christ. I answered that I didn't know how, but that I couldn't help knowing that He was beside me, that I saw and felt Him clearly, that my recollection of soul was greater, and that I was very continuously in the prayer of quiet, that the effects were much different from those I usually experienced, and that it was very clear.

I could do nothing but draw comparisons in order to explain myself. And, indeed, there is no comparison that fits this kind of vision very well. Since this vision is among the most sublime (as I was afterward told by a very holy and spiritual man, whose name is Friar Peter of Alcantara and of whom I shall speak later, and by other men of great learning) and the kind in which the devil can interfere the least of all, there are no means by which those of us who know little here below can explain it. Learned men will explain it better. For if I say that I see it with the eyes neither of the body nor of the soul, because it is not an imaginative vision, how do I know and affirm that He is more certainly at my side than if I saw Him? It is incorrect to think that the vision is like that experience of someone blind or in the dark who doesn't see the other at his side. There is some likeness in this comparison but not a great deal, because in such a case the person experiences with his senses: either he hears the other person speak or stir, or touches him. In the vision there is nothing of this, nor do you see darkness; but the vision is represented through knowledge given to the soul that is clearer than sunlight. I don't mean that you see the sun or brightness, but that a light, without your seeing light, illumines the intellect so that the soul may enjoy such a great good. The vision bears with it wonderful blessings.[9]

Henry Suso has said that "a vision is to be esteemed the more noble the more intellectual it is, the more it is stripped of all images and approaches the state of pure contemplation."[10] This is the position taken by John of the Cross. He warns of the dangers of taking "successive" locutions as direct revelations of God (these are "the words and reasonings that the spirit usually forms while recollected").[11]

> I knew someone who in his experience of these successive locutions formed, among some very true and solid ones about the Blessed Sacrament, others that were outright heresies.

> And I greatly fear what is happening in these times of ours: If any soul whatever after a bit of meditation has in its recollection one of these locutions, it will immediately baptize all as coming from God and with such a supposition say, "God told me," "God answered me." Yet this is not so, but, as we pointed out, these persons themselves are more often the origin of their locution.[12]

On the other hand where the words are more interior and effect in the substance of the soul what they signify, then they are what John of the Cross calls "substantial" words and they are to be valued because of the interior union with God that they herald. If a person hears the Lord say "Love me" and experiences within the transforming love of God, then this is such a "substantial locution."[13] John of the Cross' position is very clear: "The more interior and substantial they are, the more advantageous they are for the soul."[14]

St. John can say then that "in the measure that a person divests himself from willful attachments to the apprehensions of those stain-like figures, morals, and images—the wrappings of spiritual communications—he will prepare himself for the goods and communications they cause."[15] This distinction between the external "wrapping" and the interior "communication" is important and helpful. John of the Cross also speaks of the vision as the "curtain," the "veil" and the "rind" covering the interior communication.[16]

Recent theologians have taken this matter further. Rahner has said: "The imaginative vision which presupposes such infused contemplation is only the radiation and reflex or contemplation in the sphere of the senses, the incarnation of the mystical process of the Spirit."[17] Rahner is not denying that God could intervene in nature and produce a miraculous vision but maintaining that normally we must presume that God works through ordinary means. Ordinarily, then, we can consider that a vision (of a person who is given the grace of contemplation) is a synthesis between (1) the pre-conceptual, contemplative experience of grace and (2) the psyche of the individual.

Evelyn Underhill would agree with Rahner's comments. She comments that visionary experience is, or at least may be, the "outward sign" of an inner union with God.[18] She appeals to the analogy of an artist in her attempt to explain what occurs in a vision: "It is a picture which the mind constructs, it is true, from raw materials already at its disposal, as the artist constructs his picture with canvas and paint."[19] However, as art depends not only upon canvas and paint, but upon the beauty and truth experienced by the artist, so the genuine vision depends not only upon the psychic structure of the person but upon the real experience of grace that the vision reflects.[20]

A genuine (pre-conceptual) experience of God will manifest itself in a given individual according to the person's background, culture, interests, sensitivity, psychic health and imaginative capacity. This means that some people will be more obviously prone to have their contemplative union with God manifest itself in the imagination as visions. Others may hear words addressed to themselves or find their prayerful union with God manifesting itself in the gift of tongues.

In this explanation the external manifestation enshrines a genuine encounter with God, in a form which is shaped both by the person's union with God and by the psyche of the individual concerned. It is obvious that there can be a kind of cultural conditioning at work in this matter. There may be cultures or subcultures which are more likely than others to have their experience of God manifest itself in visions or in the gift of tongues.

To say that a vision is the result of an experience of God combined with a particular individual's psychic response is not to deny that the final outcome may be entirely providential. God may be providentially assisting the faith of others through the experience of visions, voices or tongues that occur in an individual. It is quite appropriate to believe, for example, that God's providence guides the whole process of the "Revelations" of Julian of Norwich or the "Dialogues" of Catherine of Siena. However, this does not deny that these dialogues may have occurred through original pre-conceptual experience finding expression in a unique individual's consciousness. We would have to suppose just such a providential guidance at work in authentic prophecy. In the prophets not only is there an authentic encounter with God but the expression of this in word is guided by the Spirit of God.

All that has been said above is based upon the presupposition that there is something genuine about a particular experience like a vision. There are of course "visions" which seem to have nothing to do with prayer, experiences which are the product of complicated psychic processes. They have not been the focus of attention here. Rather the question has been more: How are we to understand unusual phenomena that accompany authentic Christian prayer?

It seems that the questions raised at the beginning of this discussion can now be answered. First, experiences like visions, voices and tongues should not necessarily be presumed to be due to the direct intervention of God. Nor should they be seen necessarily as simply the product of the human psyche (although they might be simply this). They are better seen as the result of (1) God's supernatural union with the person in a preconceptual contemplative way, and (2) the "incarnation" of this in a particular individual's life.

What this means in our attitude to visions and such experiences when they occur in others is that we should hold a double attitude. On the one hand we are called to respect and reverence for the experience of grace that may well be the core of the vision. On the other hand we may well withhold judgment about the details of a vision, knowing that those are not directly of God but are influenced by the disposition of the visionary.

Furthermore there is no clear way of distinguishing what is of God and what is the product of the individual in a particular case. There is no way of knowing when a person has been guided by the Holy Spirit in the whole process of enfleshing the experience of God, except by the results and the fruits of what is expressed. What is clear both in theory and from many practical cases is that a person may be quite holy and apparently enjoying genuine experience of God and yet have visions or hear words that are quite erroneous.[21]

John of the Cross has provided us with a practical approach to these phenomena. We are always to turn our heart back to a stance of openness and waiting for the gift of God given in the darkness of faith, rather than to go seeking after such experiences which are byways from the path which leads directly to God.

ten

EXPERIENCE OF GOD AND CHRISTIAN FAITH

The final question to be addressed concerns the relationship between experience of God and growth in faith. What is the movement by which faith grows and what part does experience of God play in this? This is not meant to raise the question about the stages in the development of faith through a lifetime,[1] but rather to open up discussion of the dynamism that is always at work in the life of faith.

In the light of what has been discussed in this book it seems appropriate to suggest that the development of Christian faith depends upon the dynamic interaction of three things: our experience of our world (with experience of other persons, and of self, at the center of this), our experience of God, and the explicit word of Christian faith.

The interaction of these three components often occurs in the following way: a person (1) encounters others in the world, (2) experiences mystery and grace at the heart of the human, (3) articulates this in explicit faith in Jesus Christ and his Gospel in the believing community, (4) transcends images and concepts in contemplative moments of prayer, and (5) is impelled toward love for others in our world.

Of course the movement does not then come to rest. Involvement with people leads to new experience of grace, to a new need to listen to the word of Scripture, and to new moments of prayer. Faith might be imaged as a spiraling movement between these elements. Since not all the aspects of this movement have been fully treated in this study, it might be helpful to conclude with a sketch of the five "moments" in the normal development of faith.

The Encounter with Others in Our World

An act of knowledge or love for another being in the world is not, in itself, a dimension of faith. However it is the necessary condition for our awareness of the horizon of mystery. It is in our knowledge and love of others in our world that we encounter the grace that surrounds and upholds us.

The most fully human encounter for a human person is the meeting with another man or woman. In such a personal encounter we become more fully aware of ourselves in our own uniqueness. But it is also in such encounters of knowledge and love that the God of grace is experienced as horizon and ground for what is most personal in our lives.

Experience of Mystery and of Grace

In all our acts of knowing and loving directed toward others in our world we experience mystery in a pre-conceptual way, as the always present horizon and condition for our knowledge and love. This experience of transcendence is, then, a universal experience but it is not always noticed, or correctly interpreted. A person might even declare that he or she is an atheist, even as the person experiences what a Christian would call the mystery of grace as the horizon of all conscious activity.

There are also those times in life when transcendence breaks in upon the pattern of our lives in a noticeable way, times of abundant richness or times of limitation, when we have a sense that this or that dimension of life is given as a free gift, a gift for which we are unable to give an account.

3 *Explicit Faith in Jesus Christ*

If it were not for the revelation that has occurred in Jesus Christ we might only be able to say that what we experience is "infinite being" or "mystery." Because of Jesus we know that we can name the term of this mystery "Abba." In Jesus we know that we have access to the Father. In his death and resurrection we find forgiveness and salvation. God is united to us in the intimacy of love through the free gift of grace, the outpouring of the Holy Spirit. This grace permeates our lives and our world; this presence of the Spirit elevates our whole existence, so that when we experience transcendence in our lives, we can be sure that this transcendence opens up toward the God of Jesus Christ.

The explicit language of Christian preaching puts words around what is already in some way experienced. It interprets and illuminates the experience of transcendence. It calls us to decision concerning the God whose grace is already operating in our lives.

The propositions of Christian faith are, then, the conceptual expression of the mystery of love that we already in some way experience. They are expressions guaranteed by Jesus Christ and by his movement, the Christian Church. As faith develops there is a constant mutual interaction between personal experience of God and the communal word of faith that is shared by the whole Church.

Individual experience of God must not rest in its obscure and individual form. It has an inbuilt dynamism to reach a fully human faith. This is faith in Jesus Christ professed in the believing community. Faith, to reach its human fullness, needs to find expression in symbol, concept and word; it needs to be celebrated in the community of disciples and lived out in the world of everyday life.

Contemplative Experience of God

However faith cannot rest, either, only in its explicit and conceptual mode. There is further need for a living union with God which transcends words and concepts.

Such a movement is always a gift of God, and it occurs by God's invitation. At the same time it is part of the normal development of faith. This movement occurs when the concrete object of our attention (such as another person, or words or images in prayer) becomes transparent and our focal awareness is on God, not through intellectual knowledge but in pre-conceptual, loving awareness.

Our reflex awareness of contemplation can only occur through images and concepts. We necessarily conceptualize our experience in some way. There is always a richness to contemplative experience that exceeds the possibility of expression. However conscious reflection on contemplative experience connects our experience to a communal tradition of faith and allows what we have experienced to take hold in us more fully.

There is, then, a constant dynamism between contemplative experience and the explicit side of faith. Contemplation occurs from within the life of faith and finds expression in the communal language of faith.

The Call to Mission

It has been shown how experience of God occurs in the movement out from self to others in our world. It has its beginning in ordinary day to day events.

The experience of grace is illuminated and interpreted through the word of God. It is deepened by the union of contemplative prayer. However the word of God and the experience of contemplation send us back to our brothers and sisters. To meet the Father of Jesus in word and prayer is to be called to share his love for all, his special love for the poorest, and his will to see justice done. It is always a call to discipleship, to walking with Jesus, to living and dying in the cause of the kingdom of God.

Characteristics of the Experience of God

What has been said earlier is recapitulated here in a series of principles which may be useful in the discernment of what is truly experience of God.

1. The experience is always of the radical transcendence of God. God is always encountered as other than ourselves, and as totally beyond our grasp.

2. At the same time God is encountered in our experience of self and our experience of our world. It is an experience of an *immanent* God.

3. It is an experience of *creatureliness*. We know that we are unable to account for our own beginning or our own future and we experience our complete dependence on Another.

4. For a Christian, experience of God is *dependent upon* and in some way *derived from* Jesus' own encounter with his Father.

5. It must, then, be compatible with *Jesus' preaching and praxis* of the *kingdom of God*.

6. In the light of the revelation in Jesus Christ we know that authentic experience of God is the experience of one who is Abba, given in the Holy Spirit through Jesus crucified and exalted at the right hand of the Father. It has a *Trinitarian* structure.

7. For one who follows Jesus it will always be an experience which directs the Christian to the community of Jesus, the *Church*, in loving obedience.

8. It will bear fruit in a life lived as a following of Jesus. It involves the path of *discipleship*.

9. It will have both a *mystical* and a *social* dimension. It will direct us both toward prayer and toward our neighbor, particularly the marginalized neighbor.

10. It is a profoundly *personal* experience. Even though Christian mystics describe the intimacy of their union with God in powerful and evocative language, yet they hold back from describing the experience in terms of a merging between Creator and creature. It is not described as a loss of identity, but rather as a finding of self in the union of love.[2] The experience of God is accompanied by the experience of presence to self.

11. The experience of God has a *general* and *indistinct* character. It has a different quality to the knowledge we have of particular persons or things in our world. God is never experienced as object among other objects of human knowledge and love, but is always encountered as the horizon and the "ground" of other experiences.

12. It is always an *obscure* character. This obscurity is imaged in the theme of the cloud of unknowing and in the dark night of John of the Cross. Even when the experience is one of illumination, yet it is still obscure. As John of the Cross teaches, it may be the darkness of midnight or it may be "the tranquil night at the time of the rising dawn," but it is never full daylight.

13. The experience is so *subtle* and *delicate* that it may not be recognized for what it is. A person acclimatized only to more obvious ways of experiencing reality may not notice this kind of experience present in his or her life.

14. The experience itself (the encounter with God) is always *pre-conceptual*. Such an encounter must be objectified in consciousness (in concept, image or word) in order that we become aware of the encounter in a reflex way. However while we must interpret what we experience, yet our interpretation is not able to do full justice to what has been experienced. We are able to distinguish between our reflex interpretation and the original encounter.

15. What we experience is *indefinable* and *ineffable*. Without historical revelation our experience of mystery would remain obscure and without clear content.

16. The experience is one of *meditated immediacy*. On the one hand it has an immediate character because it is an experience of radical openness and nearness to God. God has drawn close to us by grace, and we can experience this presence without the mediations of concepts and images. On the other hand the experience is mediated in the sense that it always arises in, and depends upon, the everyday experience of people and events in our lives. Like every experi-

ence it has to be mediated in another sense: in order for us to have reflex knowledge of it this experience must find expression in our minds in concept, image or word.

17. In the encounter with God the awareness we enjoy has been well described traditionally as *knowledge through love* or *loving knowledge*. It is not intellectual comprehension but more the kind of illumination that can occur in the union of love.

18. The encounter with God is aways the experience of *gift*. The human person knows that he or she is receptive and to some extent passive in the encounter with God. God is the primary agent in the experience and the individual knows that he or she is receiving a free gift.

NOTES

1. The Scriptures are filled with texts which point to an inner experience of God. Perhaps it will suffice to point to Paul's Letter to the Romans and St. John's Gospel: "God's love has been poured into our hearts through the Holy Spirit who has been given to us" (Rom 5:5). "For all who are led by the Spirit of God are sons of God. . . . When we cry 'Abba! Father!' it is the Spirit himself bearing witness with our spirit that we are children of God" (Rom 8:14–16). "Likewise the Spirit helps us in our weakness; for we do not know how to pray as we ought, but the Spirit himself intercedes for us with sighs too deep for words" (Rom 8:26). "No one can come to me unless the Father who sent me draws him; and I will raise him up on the last day. It is written in the prophets: 'And they shall all be taught by God.' Everyone who has heard and has learned from the Father comes to me" (Jn 6:44–45). This last text from John echoes Old Testament references to an inner knowledge of God. See Is 54:13; Jer 31:33–34; Hos 11:4; Jn 6:65; 12:32.

2. The experiential dimension of faith is strong in Augustine's thought. He distinguished the things that are believed (*ea quae creduntur*) from the faith by which they are believed (*fides qua creduntur*) (*De Trinitate* 13.2.5), and taught that this personal faith can be experienced by the individual (*De Trinitate* 13.1.3), that the Trinitarian missions to the individual soul can be "known and perceived" (*De Trinitate* 4.20.28), and that there is an inner illumination and attraction of the Holy Spirit in the act of faith (*In Joannis Evangelium* 26.4–8; 106.6; 115.4; *De Gratia Christi et de Peccato Originali* 1.14–15). St. Thomas taught that there is an interior cause to faith which is God

moving the soul to believe interiorly by his grace. This he called the *lumen fidei* or the *instinctus fidei* (see *Summa Theol.* 2–2.6.1; *Evangelium Joannis* 6.5.3). While our human intellects are as little geared to the knowledge of God as is the owl's eye for the sun (*Summa Contra Gentiles* 3.25.2) yet there is a knowledge by which we are joined to God as if in unknowing (*ibid.* 3.49). Here and in other places Thomas follows Pseudo-Dionysius in his teaching that the way of unknowing constitutes the most sublime form of knowledge (*De Divinis Nominibus* 7.4; *1 Sent* 8.1.1 ad 4). Commenting on Augustine's teaching about our awareness of the inner Trinitarian missions Thomas describes this knowledge as a knowledge though love, the gift of wisdom, and he speaks of it as a quasi-experimental knowledge (*Summa Theol.* 1.43.5 ad 2; *1 Sent* 14.2.2. ad 3) and simply as experimental knowledge (*1 Sent* 15.2 ad 5; 16.1 ad 2) of the indwelling Trinity. This is discussed by John Dedek in "*Quasi Experimentalis Cognitio:* A Historical Approach to the Meaning of St. Thomas," *Theological Studies* 22 (1961):363–70.

3. Schillebeeckx makes this point strongly. For him "experience is always interpreted experience." See *Christ: The Christian Experience in the Modern World* (London: SCM, 1980), pp. 30ff.

4. *Experience and God* (London: Oxford University Press, 1968), p. 24. Smith also says: "Experience must involve encounter in the sense that the one who has the experience must be co-existent with, and at the same time stand out against, what there is to be experienced. . . . Encounter on the other hand, though necessary, is not sufficient; the actualization of experience requires not only something to be encountered, but a sign-making animal capable of making discriminations and of expressing them in appropriate language. In actual experiencing, the two ingredients—the material of encounter and the one who encounters—go together" (pp. 31–32). Dermot Lane, in his helpful book *The Experience of God: An Invitation To Do Theology* (Dublin: Veritas, 1981), also looks to John E. Smith for his description of experience.

5. See John E. Smith, *Experience and God*, pp. 21–45.

6. *Personal Knowledge: Towards a Post-Critical Philosophy* (University of Chicago Press, 1958), p. 88.

7. *Ibid.*

8. For this kind of understanding of religious experience see William James, *The Varieties of Religious Experience* (New York: Random House, 1935).

9. For an example of this see Jean Mouroux, *The Christian Experience: An Introduction to a Theology* (New York: Sheed and Ward, 1954).

10. Rahner often uses the expression this way. See his article "Reflections on the Experience of Grace," *Theological Investigations* 3, pp. 86–90.

11. See, for example, Karl Rahner in his *The Spirit in the Church* (New York: Seabury Press, 1979), p. 22. While Rahner's intention in linking everyday experience of God in life with contemplative or mystical experience is admirable, I prefer to use the word "mysticism" in a more precise way.

CHAPTER 2

1. As Rahner points out in *Foundation of Christian Faith* (New York: Seabury Press, 1978), "If we were simply to say that 'God' is the term of our transcendence, then we would have to be continually afraid of the misunderstanding that we were speaking of God in the way that he is already expressed, known and understood beforehand in an objectifying set of concepts" (p. 61).

2. For this approach to mystery see Rahner's article "The Concept of Mystery in Catholic Theology," *Theological Investigations,* 4:36–73; cf. "Mystery," *Encyclopedia of Theology: A Concise Sacramentum Mundi,* pp. 1000–1004; *Foundations of Christian Faith,* pp. 44–89.

3. The philosophical foundation for this section can be found in Rahner's *Spirit in the World* (New York: Herder and Herder, 1968). He demonstrates that whenever our intellects reach out to grasp an individual object they do so only in pre-apprehension (*Vorgriff*) which reaches out toward infinite being. This pre-apprehension of being without limits is the necessary condition for our knowledge of objects in our world.

The following paragraph from *Spirit in the World* (p. 142) puts Rahner's position clearly: "We must therefore ask how the agent intellect is to be understood so that it can know the form as limited, confined, and thus as of itself embracing further possibilities. Obviously this is possible only if, antecedent to and in addition to apprehending the individual form it comprehends of itself the whole field of these possiblities and thus, in the sensibly concretized form, experiences the concreteness as limitation of these possibilities, whereby it knows the form itself as able to be multiplied in this field. This transcending apprehension of further possibilities, through which the form possessed in a concretion in sensibility is apprehended as limited and so is abstracted, we call "pre-apprehension" (*Vorgriff*). Although this term is not to be found literally in Thomas, yet its content is contained in what Thomas calls *excessus* (excess), using a similar image."

In *Hearers of the Word*—the excerpts here are from the translation of Joseph Donceel in Gerald A. McCool (ed.), *A Rahner Reader* (New York: Seabury Press, 1975)—he shows how individual objects are known "as profiled against this absolute range of all the knowables" (p. 16). The *Vorgriff* aims at infinite being: "The *Vorgriff* intends God's absolute being in the sense that the absolute being is always basically co-affirmed by the basically illimited range of the *Vorgriff*" (p. 19).

In *Foundations of Christian Faith* Rahner returns to a discussion of the *Vorgriff*: "Man is a transcendent being insofar as all of his knowledge and all of his conscious activity is grounded in a pre-apprehension (*Vorgriff*) of 'being' as such, in an unthematic but ever-present knowledge of the infinity of reality" (p. 33). The exercise in the text is aimed at an exploration of this pre-apprehension, not through philosophical discussion, but through a personal search into our own knowing. If Rahner's insight is correct (and I believe it is) then it means that this horizon of being without limits is present (if not explicitly noticed) as the condition for all our knowing. The exercise simply aims a drawing attention to this horizon.

4. Metaphysics becomes possible, then, as a reflection on this pre-conceptual awareness of being without limit: "Metaphysics does not consist in the vision of a metaphysical object, perhaps of being as such, but the *transcendental reflection* upon that which is affirmed implicitly and simultaneously in the knowledge of the world, in the affirmation of physics" (*Spirit in the World*, p. 398).

5. I have chosen to reflect about the transcendental depths of human loving because it seems simpler and clearer than a general transcendental reflection on freedom and the will, such as Rahner undertakes in *Hearers of the Word*. For a mystagogical approach to human freedom see James J. Bacik, *Apologetics and the Eclipse of Mystery: Mystagogy According to Karl Rahner* (University of Notre Dame Press, 1980), pp. 84ff.

6. See Rahner's comments in "Reflection on the Unity of the Love of Neighbor and the Love of God," *Theological Investigations* 6:231–49.

7. On this see Rahner's articles "The Experience of God Today," *Theological Investigations* 11:149–65 and especially "Experience of Self and Experience of God," *Theological Investigations* 13:122–32.

8. Rahner's comments on the *Vorgriff* in *Hearers of the Word* make this quite clear: "Now this *Vorgriff* does not represent the infinite in himself, it only co-affirms him as the ultimate whereunto of the illuminated dynamism of the spirit that we call *Vorgriff*. On the other hand the *Vorgriff* occurs and we know about it only as the condition of the possibility of conceptual knowledge of finite objects. It seems to follow that we know of God's infinity only in connection with finite being" (p. 26).

9. This is well said in *Foundations of Christian Faith:* "The term of transcendence is indefinable because the horizon itself cannot be present within the horizon, because the term of transcendence cannot itself really be brought within the scope of transcendence and thus distinguished from other things. The ultimate measure cannot itself be measured. The limit by which everything is 'defined' cannot itself be defined by a still more ultimate limit. The infinite expanse which can and does encompass everything else cannot itself be encompassed" (p. 63).

10. Hans Küng has recently attempted to revive the classical approach in his *Does God Exist? An Answer for Today* (Garden City, New York: Doubleday, 1980). This is a persuasive book, but, it seems to me, less helpful for today than the transcendental approach of Marechal, Rahner and Lonergan.

11. This approach is also found in St. Thomas. It will be dealt

with later in this work, as an integral part of an overall theology of experience of God.

CHAPTER 3

1. There have been many recent attempts to evoke "experiences of grace," "moments of mystery" and "signals of transcendence." See, for example, James J. Bacik, *Apologetics and the Eclipse of Mystery* (University of Notre Dame Press, 1980); Peter Berger, *A Rumour of Angels* (New York: Doubleday, 1969); Leonardo Boff, *Liberating Grace* (New York: Orbis Press, 1979); Landon Gilkey, *Naming the Whirlwind* (New York: Bobbs-Merrill, 1969); Rosemary Haughton, *The Knife Edge of Experience* (London: Darton, Longman and Todd); John Macquarrie, *Principles of Christian Theology* (New York: Scribner's, 1977), pp. 53–110; Schubert Ogden, *The Reality of God* (New York: Harper and Row, 1966), pp. 21–43; Karl Rahner, *The Spirit in the Church;* John Shea, *Stories of God: An Unauthorized Biography* (Chicago: Thomas More Press, 1978), pp. 11–39; Paul Tillich, *Systematic Theology* (University of Chicago Press, 1967), pp. 11–15; David Tracy, *Blessed Rage for Order* (New York: Seabury Press, 1975), pp. 91–118. Rahner's works, beside the one book refered to above, are full of what he calls "mystagogies."

2. *Revelation of Divine Love,* trans M.L. Del Mastro (New York: Doubleday, 1977), p. 125.

3. Henri Nouwen is a contemporary spiritual writer who writes well of this movement from loneliness to solitude. See his *Reaching Out: The Three Movements of the Spiritual Life* (Garden City, N.Y.: Doubleday, 1975), pp. 13–44, and *Clowning in Rome* (Garden City, N.Y.: Doubleday, 1979) pp. 5–34.

CHAPTER 4

1. This has been thoroughly researched by J. Jeremias. See his *New Testament Theology,* Volume 1 (London: SCM, 1971), p. 61ff, and his *The Prayers of Jesus* (London: SCM, 1967), pp. 11–65. Need-

less to say, the point of Abba as an image of God is not its masculinity but the intimate love it suggests.

2. *The Prayers of Jesus*, pp. 56–57.

3. *Ibid.*, p. 60.

4. *Jesus: An Experiment in Christology* (New York: Seabury Press, 1979), p. 256.

5. *Ibid.*, p. 268.

6. As Sobrino comments: "The most certain historical datum about Jesus' life is that the concept which dominated his preaching, the reality which gave meaningfulness to all his activity, was 'the kingdom of God' " *Christology at the Crossroads: A Latin American Approach* (New York: Orbis Books, 1978), p. 41.

7. James D. G. Dunn, *Jesus and the Spirit: A Study of the Religious and Charismatic Experience of Jesus and the First Christians as Reflected in the New Testament* (London: SCM, 1975), p. 67.

8. This expression is influenced by the work of J. D. Crossan, *In Parables: The Challenge of the Historical Jesus* (New York: Harper and Row, 1973), p. 33.

9. See Hans Küng, *On Being a Christian* (Garden City, N.Y.: Doubleday, 1976), pp. 249ff. See also Schillebeeckx's whole approach in *Jesus: An Experiment in Christology*.

10. See Schillebeeckx's *Christ: The Christian Experience in the Modern World*, especially pp. 646–839.

11. Norman Perrin has shown that the kingdom must be understood as a symbol. See his *Jesus and the Language of the Kingdom: Symbol and Metaphor in New Testament Interpretation* (London: SCM, 1976).

12. Sobrino points out that there was a real history of Jesus' own faith as he responded to these events. See his *Christology at the Crossroads*, pp. 91–95.

13. *Jesus and the Spirit*, pp. 199–342.

14. *Ibid.*, p. 194.

15. *Ibid.*, p. 195.

CHAPTER 5

1. For "man as the event of God's free and forgiving self-communication," see Rahner's *Foundations of Christian Faith*, pp. 116ff.

2. This pessimistic tradition in theology runs from Augustine to Calvin to the twentieth century. In Catholic teaching it was sometimes expressed in the saying "Outside the Church there is no salvation."

3. This truth can be argued from the whole dynamism and meaning of the Old and New Testaments, but it receives its most explicit formulation in 1 Timothy 2:4.

4. For the teaching of Vatican II on this issue see *Lumen Gentium*, n. 16; *Gaudium et Spes*, n. 22; *Ad Gentes*, n. 7. Rahner judges that this doctrine "marked a far more decisive phase in the development of the Church's conscious awareness of its faith than, for instance, the doctrine of collegiality in the Church, the relationship between Scripture and tradition, the acceptance of the new exegesis, etc.": "Observations on the Problem of the 'Anonymous Christian' " *Theological Investigations* 14, p. 284.

5. *The Spirit in the Church*, p. 13.

6. *Ibid.*, p. 17.

7. For Augustine's view see his *De Trinitate* 4.2. On this area and that of the following note see the discussion above in note 2 of Chapter 1.

8. *Summa Theologiae* 1.43.5 ad 2.

9. This twofold movement of divine self-communication has again become normal in Catholic theology. See for example Karl Rahner's systematic treatment in *Foundations of Christian Faith*.

10. The argument that faith in Jesus Christ is always and necessarily mediated to us by the Christian community is well developed by Edward Schillebeeckx in the first section of his *Jesus: An Experiment in Christology*.

11. This is concisely and clearly argued by Rahner in his article on "Faith" in *Sacramentum Mundi* 2:310–13.

12. *Summa Theologiae* 2–2.6.1; *Evangelium Joannis* 6.5.3; *Quaestiones Quodlibetales* 2.4.1.

13. See Dermot Lane's comments in *The Experience of God*, p. 26.

14. See Metz's approach in his *Followers of Jesus* (London: Burns and Oates, 1978) and in his *Faith in History and Society* (London: Burns and Oates, 1980).

15. James Mackey has shown how this experience that all is gift is a key insight into Jesus' understanding of the kingdom of God. He writes beautifully of this experience: "The true value of all that exists is discovered in the unique way in which one values a gift; we should therefore not crush by grasping, or tear by trying to pull away. The gift has its roots in the giver like a flower with roots hidden that breaks ground to brighten a common day, grasp and pull it loose, and its brightness is already blighted by impending decay. The gift is the bird in the hand, held in a gesture that is more one of holding dear, as the saying goes, than one of grasping and appropriating, a gesture that embodies the ability and willingness to let go, a gesture of trust equal to the sense of having been trusted and entrusted. We should know how to enjoy without hoarding life with its supports and enrichments, its root and flower, its flesh and flight, as a loved one is possessed but cannot be owned. We should look again at the birds of the air and the lilies of the field": *Jesus the Man and the Myth: A Contemporary Christology* (New York: Paulist, 1979), pp. 159–60.

16. 1 Kings 19:11–13.

17. This is a line from stanza 13 of the poem the *Spiritual Canticle* by John of the Cross.

18. See Rahner, *Foundations of Christian Faith*, pp. 83–84, and E. Schillebeeckx, *Jesus*, p. 632.

19. "Deus qui in hac vita non potest per seipsum cognosci, potest per seipsum amari" (*Summa Theol.* 1–2.27.2 ad 2).

20. Caritas est quae, dilegendo, animam immediate Deo coniungit spiritualis vinculo unionis" (*Summa Theol.* 2–2.27.4 ad 3).

CHAPTER 6

1. See Metz's critique of privatized theology in *Faith in History and Society*, pp. 34ff.

2. The best known expression of Marx's critique appears in the *Contribution to the Critique of Hegel's Philosophy of Right:* "Religious distress is at the same time the expression of real distress and the protest against real distress. Religion is the sigh of the oppressed creature, the heart of a heartless world, just as it is the spirit of a spiritless situation. It is the opium of the people. The abolition of religion as the

illusory happiness of the people is required for their real happiness. The demand to give up the illusions about its condition is the demand to give up a condition which needs illusions. The criticism of religion is therefore in embryo the criticism of the vale of woe, the halo of which is religion. Criticism has plucked the imaginary flowers from the chain not so that man will wear the chain without any fantasy or consolation but so that he will shake off the chain and cull the living flower. The criticism of religion disillusions man to make him think and act and shape his reality like a man who has been disillusioned and has come to reason, so that he will revolve round himself and therefore round his true sun. Religion is only the illusory sun which revolves round man as long as he does not revolve round himself": *Karl Marx and Friedrich Engels on Religion* (New York: Schocken Books, 1964), p. 42.

3. There are times when Metz seems to promote this view in the opposition he sets up between a "transcendental and idealistic" and a "narrative and practical" Christianity. See his *Faith in History and Society: Towards a Practical Fundamental Theology*, pp. 154–68.

4. On the social function of religion see Peter Berger, *The Sacred Canopy: Elements of a Sociological Theory of Religion* (Garden City, New York: Doubleday, 1967).

5. Karl Rahner has commented on this: "Insofar as the critique by Metz is correct, every concrete mystagogy must obviously from the very beginning consider the societal situation and the Christian praxis to which it addresses itself. If this is not sufficiently done in my theory of mystagogy and in its explanation in this book, then this theory must be filled out. However, it is not therefore false. For it has always been clear in my theology that a transcendental experience (of God and of grace) is always mediated through a categorical experience in history, in interpersonal relationships, and in society. If one not only sees and takes seriously these necessary mediations of transcendental experience but also fills it out in a concrete way, then one already practices in an authentic way political theology, or, in other words, a practical fundamental theology. On the other hand, such a political theology is, if it truly wishes to concern itself with God, not possible without reflection on those essential characteristics of man which a transcendental theology discloses. Therefore, I believe that my theology and that of Metz

are not necessarily contradictory. However, I gladly recognize that a concrete mystagogy must, to use Metz's language, be at the same time 'mystical and political': "Introduction" to James J. Bacik, *Apologetics and the Eclipse of Mystery: Mystagogy According to Karl Rahner* (University of Notre Dame Press, 1980), p. x.

6. J. D. Crossan has gone so far as to suggest that "the basic attack of Jesus is on an idolatry of time and that this is the center whence issued forth what Yeats called that Galilean turbulence which set Jesus against all the major religions options of his contemporaries": *In Parables: The Challenge of the Historical Jesus* (New York: Harper and Row, 1973), p. 35.

7. See Berger's *The Sacred Canopy*, chapters 1 and 2.

8. Leonardo Boff has attempted to develop a theology of grace which takes due account of its social dimension. See his *Liberating Grace* (New York: Orbis Books, 1979), especially pp. 141–47. On this see also P. Fransen, "Die personale und gemeinschaftliche Struktur der menschlichen Existenz," in *Mysterium Salutis* 4/2 (Einsiedeln, 1975):939–51; J. L. Segundo, *Grace and the Human Condition* (New York: Orbis Books, 1973); Roger Haight, *The Experience and Language of Grace* (Dublin: Gill and Macmillan, 1979), pp. 143–83.

9. This echoes the twofold task of a critical theology, as understood by Latin American theologians of "annunciation" and "denunciation." See G. Gutierrez, *A Theology of Liberation* (New York: Orbis, 1973), pp. 265–72.

10. See the comment of G. Aulen: "Throughout the history of religions there has been a general rule: the more rigorously the demand is formed the more this leads to a discrimination against people of alienating behavior. In Jesus we find the direct opposite": *Jesus in Contemporary Historical Research* (London: SPCK, 1976), p. 22. On the exclusiveness of the various religious groups which existed in the time of Jesus see J. Jeremias *Jerusalem in the Time of Jesus* (London: SCM, 1969), especially pp. 147–267.

11. The masses who "do not know the law" (Jn 7:49) were referred to the *ammē hā'āres*. See Jeremias, *Jerusalem in the Time of Jesus*, p. 266.

12. See E. Schillebeeckx, *Jesus: An Experiment in Christology*, pp. 229–71.

13. See *The Dark Night* in K. Kavanaugh, O.C.D. and O. Rodriguez, O.C.D. (translators), *The Collected Works of St. John of the Cross* (Washington, D.C.: I.C.S. Publications, 1973), pp. 329–89.

14. *The Spiritual Canticle*, in *The Collected Works*, p. 471.

15. See the comments of John of the Cross in *The Dark Night:* "There is nothing in contemplation or the divine inflow which of itself can cause pain; contemplation rather bestows sweetness and delight. The cause for not experiencing these agreeable effects is the soul's weakness and imperfection at that time, its inadequate preparation, and the qualities it possesses which are contrary to this light": *The Collected Works*, pp. 349–50.

16. *Community and Growth* (Sydney: St. Paul Publication, 1979), p. 146.

17. This image is well developed by J. B. Libanio in a manuscript entitled "The Great Ruptures of Religious Life." On the general theme under discussion see Segundo Galilea, "Liberation as an Encounter with Politics and Contemplation," *Concilium* 96 (1974), pp. 19–33.

18. On this see Rahner's comments in "The Logic of Concrete Individual Knowledge in Ignatius Loyola," in *The Dynamic Element in the Church* (New York: Herder and Herder, 1964), pp. 150–51.

19. "The Prison Pastorate," in *Mission and Grace*, Vol. 3 (London: Sheed and Ward), pp. 86–87.

20. *Ibid.*

CHAPTER 7

1. The symbol, of course, emerges in the poem "The Dark Night," and the symbol and the poem stand behind the two books, *The Ascent of Mount Carmel* and *The Dark Night*. See *The Collected Works of St. John of the Cross*, translated by Kieran Kavanaugh, O.C.D. and Otilio Rodriguez, O.C.D. (Washington, D.C.: Institute of Carmelite Studies, 1979). All references will be to this edition.

2. *St. Gregory of Nyssa, The Life of Moses*, translated by Abraham J. Malherbe and Everett Ferguson (New York: Paulist Press, 1978), no. 164, p. 95. See Psalm 17:12.

3. *Ibid.*

4. See his *Theologica Mystica* 1.1. *PG* 111:997 A-1000A. This whole work is translated in *The Fire and the Cloud: An Anthology of Catholic Spirituality*, edited by David A. Fleming (New York: Paulist Press, 1978), pp. 56–61.

5. See Pseudo-Dionysius, *Theologica Mystica*, 2.

6. John of the Cross has quite a sophisticated understanding of symbolic language and its immediacy to experience. See his prologue to *The Spiritual Canticle*. For a contemporary view of this see Paul Ricoeur, *The Symbolism of Evil* (Boston: Beacon Press, 1967), and "The Hermeneutics of Symbols and Philosophical Reflection: 1," in *Paul Ricoeur; The Conflict of Interpretations, Essays in Hermeneutics*, ed. Don Ihde (Evanston: Northwestern University Press, 1974), especially p. 290. For the classic treatment of St John's symbol of the night, see Jean Baruzi, *Saint Jean de la Croix et le problème de l'expérience mystique* (Paris: Felix Alcan, 1924), p. 305.

7. "Saint Jean de la Croix . . ." p. 330.

8. *The Dark Night*, 1.9.4.

9. *Ibid.*, 1.9.8.

10. *Ibid.*, 2.5.1.

11. These lines are from stanza 14 of the poem "The Spiritual Canticle." See Kavanaugh, *The Collected Works*, p. 714.

12. *The Dark Night*, 1.8.4.

13. See *The Ascent of Mount Carmel*, 2.13; *The Dark Night* 1.9.

14. This is treated explicitly in *The Ascent of Mount Carmel*, 2.15.

15. See *The Spiritual Exercises of St. Ignatius*, translated by Louis J. Puhl, S.J. (Chicago: Loyola University Press, 1951), pp. 49ff.

16. This presentation of the three signs follows the treatment in *The Ascent of Mount Carmel* 2.13.2–4. The signs given in *The Dark Night* (1.9.2–8) allow for a more negative experience, but they are basically the same.

17. *The Ascent of Mount Carmel*, 2.13.7.

18. See his question about the damage done when spiritual directors do not recognize the delicate invitations of the Holy Spirit: "Who will succeed in repairing that delicate painting of the Holy Spirit once it is marred by a coarse hand?" John of the Cross continues: "Although this damage is beyond anything imaginable, it is so com-

mon and frequent that scarcely any director will be found who does not cause it in souls God is beginning to recollect in this manner of contemplation. How often is God anointing a contemplative with some very delicate unguent of loving knowledge, serene, peaceful, solitary, and far withdrawn from the senses and what is imaginable, as a result of which this person cannot meditate, nor reflect on anything, nor enjoy anything heavenly or earthly (since God has engaged him in that lonely idleness and given him the inclination to solitude), when a spiritual director will happen along who, like a blacksmith, knows no more than how to hammer and pound with the faculties": *The Living Flame of Love*, 3.42–43. A few paragraphs later he comments: "These directors should reflect that they themselves are not the chief agent, guide and mover of souls in this matter, but that the principal guide is the Holy Spirit, who is never neglectful of souls, and that they are instruments for directing them to perfection through faith and the law of God, according to the Spirit God gives each one" (3.46).

19. *The Ascent of Mount Carmel*, 2.15.5.

20. *The Dark Night*, 1.10.4. See also *The Living Flame of Love*, 3.33.

21. *The Dark Night*, 2.5.1.

22. *Ibid.*, 2.5.5.

23. *Ibid.*, 2.5.7.

24. *Ibid.*, 2.9.11.

25. *Ibid.*, 2.11.7.

26. *Ibid.*, 2.12.6.

27. *The Collected Works*, p. 711.

28. This explanation follows Rahner's comments on the connection between our experience of transcendence in life and St. Ignatius' "consolation without cause": "The conceptual object which in normal acts is a condition of awareness of this transcendence can also become more transparent, can almost entirely disappear, remain itself unheeded, so that the dynamism itself alone becomes more and more essential. If this transcendence is present in this way in its purity and as itself the focus of awareness, without being meditated by the conceptual object and so hidden, and if this occurs not only in cognition but also as the pure dynamism of the will in positive affirmation and receptivity, in love that is to say, then we have the lowest stage of what

Ignatius is probably referring to, without metaphysical and theological terminology, when he speaks of the consolation *sin causa*": "The Logic of Concrete Individual Knowledge in Ignatius Loyola," in *The Dynamic Element in the Church* (London: Burns and Oates, 1964), pp. 145–46.

29. Harvey Egan has applied Rahner's insight concerning the consolation without cause (CSCP) to the meditations in *The Spiritual Exercises:* "The CSCP, the non-conceptual experience of Christ affected and whither-directed subjective transcendence arises in and through the meditations on the life of Christ. Arising in and through these meditations, the CSCP reaches the goal 'demanded' of supernaturally elevated transcendence to be taken up and to surrender to the Father's loving mystery. As we shall see later on, Christ is the supreme case of the success of created self-transcendence to give itself totally to the loving Mystery which calls it out of and beyond itself. Because our subjective transcendence has been supernaturally elevated and also touched by the historical Christ, the basic dynamism of our transcendence corresponds to Christ's": *The Spiritual Exercises and the Ignatian Mystical Horizon* (St Louis: Institute of Jesuit Sources, 1976), p. 41.

CHAPTER 8

1. For a treatment of discernment in the New Testament and particularly in Paul, see the article of Jacques Guillet in the *Dictionnaire de Spiritualite* (Vol. III, cols. 1222–1291), translated in the book *Discernment of Spirits,* by Jacques Guillet, Gustave Bardy, Francois Vandenbroucke, Joseph Pegon and Henri Martin (Collegeville: Liturgical Press, 1970).

2. See F. Vandenbroucke in *A History of Christian Spirituality,* Vol. 2: *The Spirituality of the Middle Ages,* by Dom Jean Leclercq, Dom Francois Vandenbroucke and Louis Bouyer (New York: Seabury, 1968), p. 331.

3. See F. C. Copleston, *Aquinas* (Penguin Books, 1955) p. 10.

4. *De Trinitate* 4.20.28.

5. *1 Sent.* 14.2.2 ad 3; *Summa Theol.* 1.43.5 ad 2.

6. *Summa Theol.* 1.43.5 ad 2.

7. *Ibid.* English translation by T. C. O'Brien (New York: McGraw-Hill, 1976), 7:223–25.

8. *Ibid.*

9. *Ibid.*

10. *Summa Theol.* 2–2.45.2.

11. *Ibid.*

12. Number 175. The edition and translation used here is that of Louis J. Puhl, S.J., *The Spiritual Exercises of St. Ignatius* (Chicago: Loyola University Press, 1951). See p. 74.

13. Numbers 179–188, pp. 75–77.

14. Numbers 183 and 188, pp. 76 and 77.

15. See the comments of Avery Dulles in his article "Finding God's Will: Rahner's Interpretation of the Ignatian Election," in Raymond Schroth (ed.), *Jesuit Spirit in a Time of Change* (Westminster, Md.: Newman Press, 1968), pp. 9–22. See, in the same book, his article "The Ignatian Experience as Reflected in the Spiritual Theology of Karl Rahner" (pp. 23–41). Karl Rahner comments on Dulles: "I agree with Dulles, of course, when he stresses that in the concrete the three times for an election do not occur in complete separation from one another but rather signify aspects of a single election, in which all three aspects appear, though in very different intensities:" "Comments by Karl Rahner on Questions Raised by Avery Dulles," in *Ignatius of Loyola: His Personality and Spiritual Heritage: Studies on the 400th Year of His Death*, ed. Friedrich Wulf (St. Louis: Institute of Jesuit Sources, 1977), p. 293.

16. Number 316, p. 142.

17. Number 317, p. 142.

18. *Ibid.*

19. Number 322, pp. 144–45.

20. Number 331, p. 147.

21. Number 335, p. 149.

22. Numbers 333–334, p. 148.

23. Numbers 330 and 336, pp. 147 and 149.

24. Rahner discusses the question in "The Logic of Concrete Individual Knowledge in Ignatius Loyola," in *The Dynamic Element in the Church* (London: Burns and Oates, 1964), pp. 132–35.

25. *Ibid.*, pp. 145–46.

26. *Ibid.*, pp. 150–51.
27. *Ibid.*, pp. 155–56.
28. "The Ignatian Experience as Reflected in the Spiritual Theology of Karl Rahner," p. 36.
29. "The Logic of Concrete Individual Knowledge . . ." p. 166.
30. *Ibid.*, pp. 166–67. See also "Comments by Karl Rahner on Questions Raised by Avery Dulles," p. 291.

CHAPTER 9

1. See *Ascent* 2:16–32.
2. *The Ascent of Mount Carmel* 2.16.6–7. *The Collected Works*, pp. 151–52.
3. *Ibid.*, 2.8., p. 125.
4. *Ibid.*, 2.16.10, pp. 152–53.
5. This threefold distinction is used by many authors. See, for example, the summary by Evelyn Underhill in her *Mysticism: A Study in the Nature and Development of Man's Spiritual Consciousness* (New York: E.P. Dutton, 1961), pp. 273 and 281. See also Book 2 of John of the Cross' *The Ascent of Mount Carmel*.
6. *Mysticism*, p. 282.
7. For John of the Cross' view see *Ascent* 2.31.2, p. 210.
8. "In this seventh dwelling place the union comes about in a different way: our good God now desires to remove the scales from the soul's eyes and let it see and understand, although in a strange way, something of the favor He grants it. When the soul is brought into that dwelling place, the Most Blessed Trinity, all three Persons, through an intellectual vision is revealed to it through a certain representation of the truth. First there comes an enkindling in the spirit in the manner of a cloud of magnificent splendor; and these Persons are distinct, and through an admirable knowledge the soul understands as a most profound truth that all three Persons are one substance and one power and one knowledge and one God alone. It knows in such a way that what we hold by faith, it understands, we can say, through sight—although the sight is not with the bodily eyes nor with the eyes of the soul, because we are not dealing with an imaginative vision. Here all three Persons communicate themselves to it, speak to it, and explain

those words of the Lord in the Gospel: that He and the Father and the Holy Spirit will come to dwell with the soul that loves Him and keeps His commandments": *The Interior Castle* 7.1., translated by Otilio Rodriguez and Kieran Kavanaugh in Vol. 11, *The Collected Works of St. Teresa of Avila* (Washington, D.C.: Institute of Carmelite Studies, 1980), p. 430.

9. Translated by Kavanaugh and Rodriguez, *The Collected Works of St. Teresa of Avila*, Vol. 1 (Washington, D.C.: Institute of Carmelite Studies, 1976), pp. 174–75.

10. Quoted by Underhill (*Mysticism*, pp. 283–84), from *Heinrich Susos Leben und Schriften*, ed. M. Diepenbrock (Regensburg, 1825), cap. LIV.

11. *Ascent* 2.28.2.

12. *Ibid.*, 2.29.4.

13. *Ibid.*, 2.31.1.

14. *Ibid.*, 2.31.2.

15. *Ibid.*, 2.16.11.

16. *Ibid.*

17. See Rahner's work *Visions and Prophecies* collected in *Studies in Modern Theology* (London: Burns and Oates, 1965), p. 139.

18. *Mysticism*, p. 271.

19. *Ibid.*

20. Rahner comments: "The content of the imaginative vision then—although the varying proportion of the different elements will be very difficult to ascertain in any case—will inevitably represent the joint effect of the divine influence plus all the subjective dispositions of the visionary": *Visions and Prophecies*, p. 145.

21. Rahner gives many examples of visions of saints which contain "historical falsehood, theological error and distortion, and subjectivity (extending even to bad taste)." See *Visions and Prophecies*, pp. 148–53. Evelyn Underhill notes that even the greatest of visionaries could find themselves giving imaginative form to what is trivial or even to the experience of evil: "When Julian of Norwich in her illness saw the 'horrible showing' of the Fiend, red with black freckles, which clutches at her throat with its paws; when St. Teresa was visited by Satan, who left a smell of brimstone behind, or when she saw him sitting on the top of her breviary and dislodged him by the use of holy

water; it is surely reasonable to allow that we are in the presence of visions which tend toward the psychopathic type, and which are expressive of little else but an exhaustion and temporary loss of balance on the subject's part, which allowed her intense consciousness of the reality of evil to assume a concrete form": *Mysticism*, p. 270.

CHAPTER 10

1. The focus here is quite different to that of James W. Fowler. See his *Stages of Faith: The Psychology of Human Development and the Quest for Meaning* (San Francisco: Harper and Row, 1981).

2. On this see the discussion of R. C. Zaehner, *Concordant Discord: The Interdependence of Faiths* (Oxford University Press, 1970). See also the comments of Louis Bouyer in *Introduction to Spirituality* (Collegeville: Liturgical Press, 1961), pp. 287–306.